Ed Parker's

INFINITE INSIGHTS INTO KENPO

VOLUME 2

PHYSICAL ANALYZATION I

by

ED PARKER

ISBN 1-4392-3710-7

Printed in the United States of America
Library of Congress Catalog Card Number 82-72784
First Printing July, 1983
Second Printing 2009
/ Kam IV, Inc. 2006
ISBN 0-910293-10-4 (5 Volume Set)
ISBN 0-910293-03-1 (Volume 2 – cloth)
ISBN 0-910293-02-3 (Volume 2 – paper)

DELSBY PUBLICATIONS / Kam IV, Inc.
Los Angeles, California

TABLE OF CONTENTS

ACKNOWLEDGEMENTS

This text would not have been completed without the assistance of my wife, Leilani, who spent hours editing each volume; to my brother, David, and my son Edmund Jr. for their illustrations; to Charles Gonzalez for not only printing each volume, but his council and guidance as well; to Jim Grunwald for his excellent and creative color photography in producing all of my book covers as well as a number of black and white photos in each of the volumes; to Jim Mitchell for his photographic series of the basics; and to Rick Hughes, Joe Palanzo and Tom Kelly for their assistance in posing for some of the photos.

I would like to again acknowledge the help of Nikita Knatz for his cover layout consistently used on all five volumes; to Gary and Jeri Garrett along with Dave Miller for typesetting the majority of the captions; to Arnold Inouye who wrote the preface to this text; and to Curtis Wong who graciously supplied me with some of the photos in this volume. The names of others who have contributed to the completion of these texts will be acknowledged in subsequent volumes.

DEDICATION

To all Martial Artists who welcome change, who are willing to allow it to happen, and who perpetuate change to obtain perfection, I dedicate this book.

CREED

"I come to you with only Karate, empty hands, I have no weapons, but should I be forced to defend myself, my principles or my honor, should it be a matter of life or death, of right or wrong; then here are my weapons, Karate, my empty hands."

Ed Parker

ABOUT THE CREED

The above Creed has become an accepted Code for many Martial Artists. Authored by Ed Parker in March of 1957, it denotes the Martial Artist's way of life in today's environment. Time inevitably alters attitudes and convictions. Therefore, in reanalyzing the Creed, the use of the words *right* or *wrong* leaves no margin for clemency, but to defend one's self. A matter of *life* or *death* means strict adherence to survival in protecting loved ones or self even if it means death to the adversary should no alternative be left. *Principles* must be upheld and protected, for without them the very core and soul of man is valueless. *Honor* motivates a Martial Artist to action because it gives him dignity. *Empty hands* (as well as other body weapons) are the substitutes that a Martial Artist uses in place of man made weapons to sustain his honor. Discipline developed through training without weapons implants justice and discretion when applying the Martial Arts. Thus the above Creed acts as a regulatory guide in aiding the Martial Artist in developing a keen sense of justice.

PREFACE

For most of us, the name "Ed Parker" is synonymous with such titles as: "Father of American Karate"; Master of Kenpo; High Priest and Prophet of the Hollywood Sect; scholar; Innovator and many others. Mr. Parker's achievements and contributions to the martial arts industry have been chronicled in news articles, magazines and books worldwide. It would take a complete volume to adequately discuss the exceptional accomplishments of this man and the great impact he has had on the innovation and advancement of American Kenpo, and Karate as a whole. However, we are indeed fortunate that Mr. Parker in his infinite wisdom saw the need for the development of a comprehensive writing which would provide Kenpo students with insights to his Art of American Kenpo. As a culmination of his many years of dedication, and of sacrifice, the first two volumes of his works entitled "Infinite Insights Into Kenpo" have been published, with volumes 3, 4, and 5 to follow. These texts provide us the base from which we may develop a clearer understanding of our movement. It is with sincere gratitude that I express my thanks to our Master for his efforts and look forward to his continuing endeavors to share his knowledge with all of us.

Generally, the expression of thanks would be the closing statement in most prefaces, however, I would like to impart to you, the readers, a side of Ed Parker "the man" which has not properly been discussed. Ed Parker is a peoples man. Those of you who have had the opportunity to participate in, or just attend, any of his lectures or seminars need not be told of this man's energies in communicating and sharing with all practitioners his philosophy on life and the principles of the art he teaches. It is with zest that the Master of our system has always held in high regard the accomplishments of his students and their efforts to project his teachings to others. He was never one to hold back praise or encouragement to any person striving to improve their art form. Many individuals in the martial arts world have come to him for advice and counsel, for which he has never asked anything in return. Ed Parker's role as a "Pioneer of American Karate" has been a guiding influence in the lives of martial artists and he continues to

v

assist and advise when called upon. As a result, the demands on our Master's time are unending and it is an amazement to those near him how he can maintain such an arduous schedule. It is in consideration of his sincere efforts to share his knowledge with dedicated practitioners that I feel the need to relate to you some of the incredible and unexplainable actions taken by people who have availed themselves of his knowledge and trust. These are individuals who have ridden the crest of Ed Parker American Kenpo only to take advantage of the opportunity to gain for themselves a status and notoriety in the martial arts world at the expense of Ed Parker. It is the deception used by these few individuals which concerns me the most. They are the very people who, in befriending Ed Parker, have used his wealth of knowledge and desire to help, by publishing their own articles and texts promoting their supposed expertise. Others have utilized their close relationship with Master Parker to promote their own personal gains. Then there are those who have gone so far as to become "new-born critics" of the man to whom most of them owe their knowledge of Kenpo. And finally, there are those individuals whose only goals in life seem to be centered on attempting to discredit the achievements of the Master of our system. The rumormongers are a prime example of this type of individual. There seems to be an unending circle of stories relating to our lineage through our Master, Ed Parker. I, for one, suggest that anyone doubting our lineage purchase Volume One of Mr. Parker's works for an education in our Kenpo heritage. As a student of American Kenpo under Master Parker, I can only hope that the types of individuals I have previously mentioned will eventually fade into the mist from which they came and that the dedicated students and instructors will continue to strive to improve themselves and the system they practice through Ed Parker's guidance. And I believe it is time to express our support and respect to the man responsible for the art we practice today. It goes without saying that Edmund K. Parker, is, American Kenpo, he is the Master of our system, and I am confident that through his strength, wisdom and experience we will all benefit from his teachings. Again, I would like to express my gratitude to our Master, Ed Parker for allowing me the opportunity to comment. It is my fondest wish for his continuing successes, now, as well as in the future.

Arnold Inouye

CHAPTER 1
INTRODUCTION

Volume II is part of an eleven year endeavor to consolidate my concepts, principles, theories, analogies, equations and beliefs regarding *American* Kenpo. Although my files are filled with partially completed as well as completed manuscripts, I felt that I had gathered enough information to adequately cover most of the essential subjects. Confident that I had meaningful material to share with the Martial Arts World, I was anxious to publish my five volume series of *Infinite Insights into Kenpo*. I have organized the material into what I feel is a logical and sequencial order of priorities to insure reader comprehension. Prioritized subjects in their proper order is a means of increasing retention.

The task of organizing material in a logical sequence is not easy. As much as I tried to condense related subjects and topics into one volume, I found it difficult. I had to constantly take the reader's point of view in order to develop a logical sequencial order. This volume, subtitled "Physical Analyzation", had to be divided into two segments. Part I is found in Volume II and Part II in Volume III. Although the topic is adequately covered, it would require five to six volumes to detail it out in total. Needless to say, the information in Volumes II and III has been structured to create interest in viewing related facets of the Art from new and varied perspectives.

Volumes II and III technically describe the **BASIC** fundamentals in the five major categories that comprise *American* Kenpo. Volume II specifically teaches you how to tailor **STANCES** to your physical make-up. Tailoring **STANCES** to each body type not only solidifies balance, but insures instant **MANEUVERABILITY. MANEUVERS** constitute the second **BASIC** topic in Volume II. Learning the numerous methods of **MANEUVERING** teaches you instantaneous *transitional response.* Stances and body postures can be quickly altered when they are coordinated with defensive and offensive movements. Thorough knowledge of **MANEUVERING** aids the transitional flow thus causing peak performance if you are in an altercation. Strategies of escape and attack are made much easier

1

when you have mastered your **STANCES** and **MANEUVERS** because they teach you the value of angle changes and how to properly use them to your advantage.

While it could be said that there is really nothing new in terms of concepts and principles, combinations of the old can be so structured and added to other fields of endeavor that they do give the appearance of new and original ideas. Rearranging the old concepts and principles in a new subject or field can often give deeper insight to a topic that would otherwise have been dull and uninteresting. More importantly, it can turn an impractical maneuver into a practical and functional response.

Breaking the bonds of tradition has truly enriched my understanding of the Martial Arts. It has given me insights that others have not been able to perceive. As stated by *Addison*, "Tradition is an important help to history, but its statements should be carefully scrutinized before we rely on them." Logic as it applies to the times is the key. In fact, an ounce of logic can be worth more than a ton of tradition that has become obsolete through the weathering of time. It would be wrong to say that we cannot learn from tradition, but to be practical, we must not let it be an all encompassing authority. On the other hand, do not overlook the wisdom that lies in men outside of your field. All men, no matter who they are or how much they know, can share their knowledge with one another. I have learned a great deal from errors made by students. Working with their mistakes has enabled me to find solutions to a number of problems. "The man who *knows how* will always be a student, but the man who *knows why* will maintain his position as the instructor."

While the ignorant refuse to study and the intelligent never stop, we should always be mindful of the fact that our reward in life is proportionate with the contributions we make. A true Martial Artist is not one who fears change, but one who causes it to happen. To live is to change, and to obtain perfection is to have changed often. Progress is a necessity that is part of nature. While it is true that casting the old aside is not necessary in order to obtain something new, we should study old theories not as a means of discrediting them, but to see if they can be modified to improve our present conditions. A word of advice, "The humble man makes room for progress; the proud man believes he is already there." Progress requires charting your course toward a successful journey to the world of ideas.

2

CHAPTER 2
HISTORY OF AMERICAN KENPO
(continued)

Teaching Kenpo in the continental United States in 1954 was not easy. Knowledge of Kenpo, Karate, Kung-Fu and other related oriental forms of pugilism was basically unknown to the American public. As a result, challenges were commonplace and comparable to the days of the old western gunfights. While every effort was made to circumvent these challenges, there were times when words alone were not sufficient. These encounters were not pleasant, but necessary for survival. As newspaper, magazine, television and movie coverage expounded on the merits and effectiveness of the Martial Arts, two conditions emerged: (1) more instructors opened schools and, therefore, challenges became more evenly dispersed thus lessening the burden for those of us who were pioneer instructors; and (2) in addition, knowledge of the effectiveness of the art deterred others from even attempting a challenge.

As my clientele increased in Pasadena and Beverly Hills (at the Beverly Wilshire Health Club) I expanded my teaching to the homes, locations, and offices of such celebrities as Blake Edwards, Robert Wagner, MacDonald Carey, Nick Adams, Elvis Presley, Joey Bishop, Jose Ferrer, Joe Hyams and others. These celebrities were instrumental in accelerating Martial Art expansion. As tournament interest increased, many of them assisted me in giving out awards at not only my tournaments, but other tournaments as well. This, naturally, added interest to our events. Blake Edwards helped me usher in the first 1964 Internationals in Long Beach, California (see photo), where Bruce Lee was first introduced to the Martial Arts world. Nick Adams and Robert Culp (see photos) were also frequent guests at the Internationals. I also invited Robert Culp (see photo) and Bruce Lee to attend Jhoon Rhee's Nationals in Washington, D.C. In addition Bruce Lee and I attended Henry Cho's tournament in New York City. Celebrity participation did indeed contribute to boosting spectator attendance. It was the responsibility of the tournament promoter to then capture the interest of the audience and educate them regarding the Martial Arts. It was important to make the audience aware that

P-1 Blake Edwards, Mike Stone, and Ed Parker at the first International Karate Championships in 1964.

P-2 Tak Kubota, Nick Adams, Ed Parker and Fumio Demura at the first International Karate Championships in 1964.

P-3 Ed Parker with Robert Culp who presented awards at the International Karate Championships.

P-4 Robert Culp in attendance at Jhoon Rhee's National Championships in Washington D.C. as a favor to Ed Parker.

the Martial Arts offered not only self-defense, but essentially builds confidence, character and a healthy self-image as well. In retrospect, proper and calculated exposure inevitably causes neophyte spectators to seek enrollment at a school close to where they live.

There were many personal fringe benefits resulting from knowing celebrities in the movie industry. As a result, I became technical advisor, stuntman, stunt choreographer on television and movie productions as well as playing the role of a character actor. The more I became involved with the Hollywood sect the more publicity I received to gain public awareness about the merits of the Martial Arts. I was, therefore, pleased when Time Magazine featured an article about my activities with the Hollywood sect (see article).

During this time period (1960-1961) Black Belt Magazine was just an idea conceived by Edmund Jung. Jung had approached me to ask my opinion about embarking on such a venture. He and the Uehara brothers (James and Mito) were discouraged by traditional Martial Artists who had told them to abandon their plans. When my opinion was sought, I encouraged Jung and made a commitment to assist him by featuring my celebrity students in his first and subsequent issues (see photo of Nick Adams and myself in their first issue). Black Belt Magazine's first issue bares record of this fact. I knew that the magazine would be successful as long as it encouraged, aided and cultivated the needs and desires of the American practitioners.

Edmund Jung went so far as to offer me one-third of the stock of Black Belt Magazine for a very minimum investment. I turned his offer down for two reasons, (1) I knew nothing about the Magazine business and in addition, journalism was not one of my main interests; and (2) I knew that the fewer the people involved in ownership of a magazine the greater its success ratio. This fact was substantiated when the two Uehara brothers bought Jung out and later felt it would be more feasible to pursue separate avenues of endeavor in the Martial Arts industry. Mito stuck with the magazine and James with the Martial Art Supply Company. Both are presently successful entrepreneurs of this ever expanding market.

As interest in the Martial Arts grew, there were many instructors I assisted along the way. Dan Ivan for one, was a recruiting officer for the Army and was indecisive as to whether he should re-enlist or try to run his Aikido and Karate school as a civilian. I talked him out of re-enlisting and aided him in supplying him with mats and other equipment necessary to conduct business on a professional level. Dan has become very successful as a Martial Arts businessman and has authored several books as well.

Takayuki Kubota of Japan contacted me about attending the 1964 Internationals in Long Beach. He desired to compete as a contestant

White House Economist
WALTER W. HELLER

Bill Bridges
TV's JASON & KARATE INSTRUCTOR PARKER
Too rough for the G.I.s.

Violent Repose

Rarely had Hollywood, which knows something about such things, witnessed such a spectacle of eye gouging, groin kicking and neck chopping. To a lavishly mirrored studio on Los Angeles' South La Cienega Boulevard last week came a pack of TV and film stars to watch an exhibition of the latest fad in craze-crazy filmland: karate. A more violent cousin of jujitsu and judo, Japanese-imported karate (pronounced kah-rah-tay) aims at delivering a fatal or merely maiming blow with hand, finger, elbow or foot, adopts the defensive philosophy that an attacker deserves something more memorable than a flip over the shoulder. Karate is now taught in more than 50 schools across the U.S., has an estimated 50,000 practitioners. But nowhere has it caught on more solidly than in Hollywood, where disciples seek tranquillity in its rigid discipline and authority.

Better Board than Head. Karate has won the allegiance of such as Actors Rory Calhoun, Macdonald Carey, Nick (*The Rebel*) Adams and TV Detectives Frank Lovejoy, Darren McGavin, and Rick (*Dangerous Robin*) Jason. Elvis Presley, who learned the sport in Germany as a G.I., now spars with two sidekicks during moviemaking lulls, and even Film Composer Bronislaw Kaper has taken to the loose white *gi* suit worn for karate lessons. Says Hollywood Columnist Joe Hyams: "We all work in an environment that's fraught with hostility. It's great to bust a board instead of a head."

Board busting with the naked hand is a spectacular but comparatively recent demonstration of karate (literally, empty hands). Legend holds that the sport was started in the 6th century by an Indian Buddhist monk named Daruma Taishi, who taught it to Chinese monks. It was refined on Okinawa after 1600, introduced in the 1920s to Japan, where it quickly shared popularity with the gentle art of jujitsu and its systematized variation, judo. But where their aim is to use an opponent's own weight to throw him to the floor without necessarily injuring him, karate aims at increasing its user's own strength to kill or injure an adversary by striking him at any of 26 vital points—chiefly with the toughened edge of the hand or the clenched fist. Although used by Japanese troops during World War II, karate is considered too ferocious for the U.S. armed forces. Nor do municipal police forces take regular karate training. "In no court," said one police official, "would karate be called 'reasonable force' in subduing a prisoner."

14-Karate King. The high priest of Hollywood's fast-growing karate sect, and host at last week's exhibition, is a blackmaned, 6-ft., 210-lb. devout Mormon named Ed Parker, who, he says, learned the deadly, lightning-fast ballet in his native Honolulu in order to avoid getting into fights with friends who taunted him because he did not drink or smoke. After serving a Coast Guard hitch during the Korean War and graduating from Brigham Young University in Provo, Utah, he moved to Pasadena, opened his first karate studio four years ago, started a second in January. He frowns upon any ostentatious use of karate, prefers to ram his fist through ten corrugated roof tiles in the privacy of his studio.

P-5a Article about Ed Parker and Rick Jason featured in "Time" magazine dated March 3, 1961.

7

Black Belt

50c

VOL. I, NO. 1   THE MAGAZINE OF SELF-DEFENSE

● JUDO ● KARATE ● AIKIDO ● KENDO

SPECIAL JUDO ISSUE
Complete National AAU Finals

P-5b&c First cover and issue of Black Belt Magazine which featured Ed Parker and Nick Adams, star of "The Rebel" television series.

confident in the knowledge that it is not necessary to prove his might or manhood. A trained Karateist possesses an abundance of self-restraint and assurance. It is a matter of record that most Karateists have gone through life without ever having to resort to its use.

Notwithstanding, Ed Parker now has reason to regard the future of Karate in this country with optimism. His ability, his adamant refusal to deviate from its strict tenets and philosophies and his forthright teaching of the science have won him acclamation and the respect of people in all walks of life. Today his mirrored studio is the scene of classes which include lawyers, doctors and other professional men who are aware of the value of the art. Some of Hollywood's best known personalities, MacDonald

Carey, Nick Adams, Rick Jason, Darren McGavin, among others, attend his sessions regularly. His advice and knowledge are sought by film studios now becoming aware of Karate's true meaning.

Unlike some instructors who profess to be experts Parker minimizes the sensational and melodramatic aspects of Kenpo Karate. Where others, in order to appeal to some pugnacious facets of human nature, declare that they teach "the art of killing" or "make you a master of anyone," he concerns himself with the truisms of Karate. His goal is to enable his students to reap the benefits it endows.

Karate is a skill that requires time and thought. One who intends to use it aggressively is only disillusioning himself. He declares that the end product of his training has al-

22

23

8

and demonstrator and also to become a resident of the United States. I introduced him to a close friend, John Nita, and asked John to be Kubota's sponsor. As a result, Kubota was able to establish a school here in the United States. Kubota did put on a memorable demonstration (at the International) pounding his shins with a sledge hammer with no apparent effects and performing a Kata. His performance attracted students who I helped find him when he opened his school. I later assisted Kubota to successfully conduct a tournament. For his first tournament, he made a substantial profit. He is now a success in his own right.

My knowledge and experience in conducting tournaments also enabled me to help Chuck Norris present a successful tournament in Las Vegas, Nevada. Here again my basic formula worked in making a profit, as opposed to having a financial disaster. While the number of contestants anticipated was there, the number of spectators present was what I had also predicted.

Traveling to tournaments around the country afforded me the opportunity to observe the talents of Mike Stone. He was from Hawaii, my native land, and I, therefore, took a shine to him. A typical Island boy, he took advantage of every opportunity open to him during a match. We sat and talked at tournaments and he revealed his plans to work for me after he received his discharge from the Army. I did accommodate him. He worked and lived with me in Pasadena, California for two to three months before approaching me with the proposition of staking him to open his own school. This I did in addition to sharing my business acumen with him to insure his success. Mike's exploits are now history, but he has without doubt made a name for himself (see photo of Mike and myself).

Developing the Martial Arts in terms of organization, content, public relations, etc. did require the help of others. One of the people who assisted me in this area was Mills Crenshaw, one of my first Utah Black Belts whom I had taught at Brigham Young University. He had been exposed to my thoughts on Kenpo and my desire to sophisticate many of the basics. Although Kenpo is a scientific and sophisticated art requiring skill which eventually bestows rank, this, we felt, was not adequate. We wanted to accord I.K.K.A. Black Belts with more prestigious titles over and above their well earned rank. It was, therefore, agreed that Black Belt ranks in our organization would be additionally distinguished by initials appropriate to each rank --comparable to a Doctor who attaches MD, DDS, or PHD to his or her name. We felt that Black Belts should be able to do this because they had obtained sophisticated knowledge and skill requiring untold hours of concentrated effort. Thus the following initials were attached to each Black Belt's signature as an optional designation of their rank in the I.K.A. Following his signature and/or designated rank one can attach the initials:

1. JI (Junior Instructor) if he or she is a first degree Black Belt.
2. AI (Associate Instructor) for a second degree Black Belt.
3. HI (Head Instructor) for a third degree Black Belt.
4. SI (Senior Instructor) for fourth degree Black Belts.
5. AP (Associate Professor) for fifth degree Black Belts.
6. P (Professor) if one is a sixth degree Black Belt.
7. SP (Senior Professor) for those who are seventh degree Black Belts.
8. AMA (Associate Master of the Arts) if an eighth degree Black Belt.
9. MA (Master of the Arts) if a ninth degree Black Belt.
10. SMA (Senior Master of the Arts) if a tenth degree Black Belt.

It was apparent from the success of the 1964 Internationals that the Martial Arts in California and the rest of the nation was destined to become popular. The ensuing years proved this to be true with the

P-6 Photo of audience at the first International Karate Championships in 1964. Over 1,000 spectators were turned away at the door.

rapid growth of Martial Art schools throughout the nation. My awareness of this trend led me to create a second tournament as well as opening a second school in the State of California. Again the location and time of year was important in planning for this second large tournament. I had purposely chosen Long Beach for the I.K.C. as a summer attraction and because it allowed practitioners to plan their vacations around this event. The first weekend of August was established as a set yearly schedule. Long Beach was selected because of its proximity to the ocean -- an anticipated deterrent to combat the summer heat and because of its close distance to a number of vacation attractions such as Disneyland, Sea World, Knotts Berry Farm and others (all are within a radius of 5 to 8 miles). In short, summer relaxation and sightseeing attractions were considerations of enticement in stabilizing attendance.

Because of the ever increasing need for tournament competition in the State of California (1/5 of the nation's total Martial Arts population during the sixties), San Francisco was my choice for a second large tournament or State Championship. I concluded that the time of the tournament should be approximately six months from the date of the Internationals. Therefore, February or March was the logical time to have this statewide tournament.

I asked Ralph Castro (who had obtained his Black Belt from me) to be my partner and together we named the tournament the "California Karate Championship". With my knowledge and experience in conducting tournaments and with the assistance of Ralph and his students, the tournament was a tremendous success bringing Ralph the notoriety anticipated. Like the Internationals in Long Beach, the C.K.C. also developed into a two day event to accommodate the large number of competitors that participated in it.

While the success of the Internationals continues today, the C.K.C., although a success for nine consecutive years ended abruptly. Circumstances beyond my control caused its downfall. Since it laid dormant for a period of five years, other tournaments in the area have taken over the California reins with success in spite of Ralph Castro's attempt to reactivate the C.K.C. independently.

Many of the nations greatest Karate champions stemmed from the Internationals and also the C.K.C. Because of the magnitude of the Internationals, grand champions became overnight successes in the Karate world. With their newly acquired reputation, the demand for their presence at other tournaments gave them great prominence. Mike Stone, Chuck Norris, Joe Lewis, Darnell Garcia, Steve Sanders and others were International champions who were in constant demand not only individually, but as members of teams representing the West Coast. I took several of these champions (Joe Lewis, Ron

11

Marchini, Ralph Castellanos, Steve Sanders and others) with me to New York to participate in tournaments on several occasions. These tournaments were billed as the East Coast versus the West Coast

P-7   Members of the West and East Coast Teams in the late 1960's.

promoted by Aaron Banks. I also conducted two team tournaments in Hawaii -- the Mainland versus Hawaii (see tournament logo and photos). The first of these tournaments was a huge success with Elvis Presley and Ricardo Montalban in attendance (see photos). The

I-1   Logo used for the United States versus Hawaii team in 1968.

12

P-8 1968 MAINLAND TEAM...(clockwise from trophies)
Mike Stone; Arnold Urquidez; Ron Marchini; Allen Steen; Chuck Norris;
Ed Parker, sponsor; Skipper Mullins; Tonny Tullener; Jerry Taylor; Greg
Baines. Not shown are: Carlos Bunda; Tom LaPuppet and 'Steve' Sanders.

P-9 1968 ALL HAWAII KARATE TEAM...
Back row: Glen Oyama, Delroy Griffith, unknown, unknown, Homer
Leong & Robert Yagi. Front row: Stanley Sugai, Toshio Ikehara, Edgar
Battad, Davis Arita, Mike Vesser, Harold Arakaki & Coach Patrick
Nakata.

P-10 Ricardo Montalban signing autographs for fans at the 1968 Hawaii Tournament of Champions.

P-11 Elvis Presley and entourage enjoying the 1968 Hawaii Tournament of Champions.

cooperative efforts of the instructors in Hawaii were more than I could hope for. The second tournament, however, was just average in size. Because of internal politics, the tournament lacked the cooperation it received the first year. Although I looked forward to this being an annual event, giving me a set time each year to visit Hawaii, I discontinued holding these tournaments after the second year. Besides, the work involved in preparing for the tournament did not allow me to enjoy my stay with my family in Hawaii while I was there. Other promoters followed, but they too abandoned their plans to continue this event.

I-2 Historical montage of the past and present drawn by Ed Parker's brother David Parker.

CHAPTER 3
PHYSICAL PREPARDNESS

Although preventive planning can in itself be your first counter AGAINST ATTACK, PHYSICAL PREPAREDNESS is necessary when you are involved IN AN ATTACK. PHYSICAL PREPAREDNESS entails the conditioning and developing of the muscles, joints, and other parts of the body so that they function with maximum proficiency in the midst of an attack. While it is true that the Art produces maximum efficiency with minimum effort, training is a prerequisite for proficiency. Proper training allows for maximum control over all mobile parts of the body. Training, however, should commence with progressive conditioning. Building the muscle tissues gradually eliminates the possibility of tearing muscle tissues. Nevertheless, while conditioning, always seek those exercises that will contribute to your stamina and reach, plus striking and kicking power. Never cheat on your exercises, but rather extend or contract your movements to the fullest extent. Keep your muscles limber. This allows you to maneuver and perform your technique with greater speed. Through conscientious and unceasing effort, maximum results can be achieved, with a minimum of expended effort, if you are ever involved in an attack.

In order to achieve these results, your training schedule should include warm ups, loosening, stretching, and strengthening exercises in addition to those that will improve your wind and reaction time. Some of the basic exercises would be side bends, head rotations, leg squats, leg stretches (see pre-stretching exercises on page 24), push ups, pull ups, leg raises, V-ups, sit ups, standing jumps, running in place and in the open, and others. (See Page 26.)

Prior to doing the exercises themselves, it would be best that we commence with a study of the muscles and their function.

THE MUSCLES AND THEIR FUNCTIONS

THE FUNCTION OF THE MUSCLE - is to contract upon being given a signal from the nervous system. Just how this takes place is an uncertainty of the anatomical mechanisms involved in the transmission of nerve impulses. Even physiologists insist that as yet there is no adequate explanation for the mechanism of muscular contractions. However, one fact is known, it is through muscle fibers that work is accomplished. Then too, it is the amount of work assigned to them in quantity, quality, and duration that determines flabbiness or development.

MECHANICS OF MOVEMENT - no one muscle acts alone in bringing about movement. In order to produce movement, it may take one or more muscles to contract the movement, another to guide its direction, a third to "hold" some part of the body so that the acting muscles will have a firm support to pull on, and fourth to stop a movement from over extending. Further, some muscles are capable of producing speed while others produce strength. Muscles must therefore work together, in various combinations, to produce control, speed, or power. No one muscle can produce all of these facets.

MUSCLE TONE - is that state of a muscle in which some of the fibers are in constant contraction thus giving it a quality of firmness. It is "muscle tone" that is essential in building strength and endurance. "Muscle tone" greatly reduces fatigue and aids the muscles in swinging into action quickly because of the fact that there is little slack to be taken up. A similar comparison can be made when comparing it to a train. When the engine begins to pull on a number of coaches, it must go at an appreciable speed before the coaches in the rear can be set in motion. As the slack of each coach is overcome by inertia, they then act as one unit following the pull of the engine. The less slack that needs to be taken up, the faster all of the coaches will quickly swing into action. However, tone can be lost through lack of exercise as well as poor diet (prevent this from happening if it is within your power).

18

STRENGTH - to have muscle strength is to have power. Muscle power, however, is not necessarily proportionate with size. Through continuous exercise, more muscle fibers are brought into action. It is the bringing together of these muscle fibers that produce more power. There are several other benefits derived from exercising the muscles: (1) it makes better use of your food supply; (2) it increases your capacity to store food fuel in larger quantities; and (3) it helps you to utilize a greater supply of oxygen. Remember, muscle power alone is not enough. It must be used intelligently, and thus, mechanical efficiency is determined.

COORDINATION - involves nerve impulses that order action, selects particular muscles to act, and determines the amount and sequence of their action. Although coordination can be developed through training and practice, learning, nevertheless, comes easily for some and with more difficulty for others. In some cases, coordination is inherited as well as instinctive. This is why some have strength and endurance, but yet lack skill, while others are obviously gifted with it. Through consistant training and practice, skill can be achieved, to a degree, by those with poor motor ability. Along with practice, a thorough understanding of what muscles are employed, how they function, and seeing them demonstrated properly, can speed up the learning process. One must be made to realize that rarely, if ever, does a muscle act alone in producing a movement. It takes several muscles acting together to produce a skillful performance. A good instructor can and should analyze each muscular activity and be able to convey his knowledge by breaking it down into its fundamentals. He should criticize and suggest whenever and wherever necessary. It is his job to get a less skilled student to that point of his training where his actions will produce satisfactory results. Muscular movements become efficient when they are executed usefully, economically, and gracefully.

FLEXIBILITY - means to increase the range of motions which are possible in a joint. Exactly what happens in the tissues of a joint is not known. Flexibility, however, can be accomplished by stretching or elongating tense, shortened muscles. To assure flexibility, especially with beginners, movements should not be forced. A beginner should commence with free rhythmical action with properly timed relaxation periods. As a student progresses, more vigorous momentum should be included. In time, the movements should be regulated to the

19

satisfaction of the individual. (The pre-stretching exercises in Volume III should be a great aid to you in developing flexibility.)

AGILITY - is dependent upon the development of sufficient flexibility and strength in performing the desired movements and the coordination to do them skillfully and easily. It may be developed through participating in activities that demand quick motor responses.

MUSCLE SORENESS - can come about through continuous and/or frequently repeated "all out" contractions or through long and continued holding of the muscles. Soreness, stiffness, or injury to muscle fibers can come about through contractions that are violent in nature. When this occurs, fibers can stretch, tear or even rupture--thus producing a condition known as "muscle strain". A more indepth study reveals that with each muscle contraction, the blood supply to the fibers is reduced. Such a reduction, if continued, renders pain or at least sensations of pain because of poor oxidation from the low count oxygen supply. Another cause of discomfort stems from the accumulation of waste products which often produce changes in the fiber. In this case of pain and discomfort, "muscle soreness" is the term used to describe it. As the muscle works, fluid from the blood collects in it. When this occurs, it may take some time after the muscle ceases to work before this excess fluid is carried away. In cases where the accumulation is excessive, it may cause the muscles to swell--thus causing "muscle stiffness". To remedy this condition, heat should be applied and a limit placed upon the muscle used. Whether taking advantage of a hot shower, using a heating pad or lamp to repair the injured fibers, "muscle soreness" need not cause alarm. Just look upon it as being a strenuous muscular activity. Like ordinary fatigue, it merely causes discomfort and is an indication that the muscle was not in the condition that it should have been in to meet the demand placed upon it.

We have certainly come a long way in perfecting our methods of training as compared to the period of the old masters. And yet, while many of their training methods are now obsolete, one cannot help but admire their relentless pursuit to achieve peak conditioning and unbelievable strength and power. Also, although they varied in their methods of training, their principles and aims were primarily the same. Realizing that both strength and power were needed in an emergency, in addition to skill and speed, they sought to develop power by using crude equipment to overcome resistance. Since weights were a simple and available form of resistance, they used this means to gain strength, and improve their athletic ability in addition to exercising without equipment. Their make shift methods included attaching two stone weights or buckets of weights to the ends of a wooden pole. It resembled a crude barbell and supplied the activity needed by the body to acquire overall power. Wrist and ankle bands made of iron were also used. After attaching these iron bands to the wrists and ankles, they proceeded to go through their basic strikes, kicks and selected maneuvers. When the bands were detached, their strength and speed was vastly improved.

A good example of a crude but effective means of developing power was once explained and demonstrated to me by a Chinese friend. He would crumple a fair sized piece of butcher paper daily and then flatten it out on the surface of a table using outward strokes of the palms. He did this exercise fifteen minutes a day over a period of years. One day while he was in the middle of a congested football crowd, he pushed both hands out in opposite directions and I was amazed to see a fair sized pathway open up in the middle of the vast gathering. Because of his persistence, he had developed tremendous strength in his forearms and triceps.

While there are many stories and examples of power derived from physical conditioning, some of the stories that have been told about the old masters have been exaggerated so that their authenticity is very doubtful. However, through conscientious and unceasing effort, you too can develop this power which is believed by the old masters to be the first stage in achieving proficiency in self-defense.

We should feel very fortunate that the physical culture field has taken tremendous scientific strides. In part, this can be credited to the efforts of the late masters. Building upon their past experiences as well as others, we have been able to have a more efficient means of body conditioning. With improved methods and equipment, the time expended is now used to greater advantage. Born with individual physical potentialities, each problem should be handled separately-- thus immensely benefiting the participant. This especially applies to cases where corrective exercises are necessary. Even the weight attachments are now detachable and interchangeable--a vast improvement over the crude stationary stone weights used in Asia centuries ago. Such an improvement allows for progressive conditioning in weight resistance.

May I remind you to build your muscle tissues gradually to eliminate the possibility of torn tissues. As already stated, when developing the muscles, remember that it is not the size of the muscle that counts, but rather the strength, stamina, and reach that you add to it. Always use those exercises that will contribute to your stamina and reach, plus striking and kicking power. Never cheat on your exercises, but rather extend or contract them to the farthest extent of your moves. Keep your muscles limber. This allows you to maneuver and perform your techniques with greater speed.

Without **PHYSICAL** training, **MENTAL** training would be of little value. While a trained *mind* enhances *physical* moves, it is limited in and of itself. Marriage of the *mind* and *body* is imperative if success is to be guaranteed in combat. But, before such a marriage is consumated, each move must be developed to its highest level before it can be compatibly united. **PHYSICAL** skills must develop to the level of *conditioned response*. The **MIND** must be developed so that the *conscious* **MIND** transposes into the *subconscious* **MIND** automatically. During this *super conscious* state, the highest level of the **SPONTANEOUS STAGE** (see Volume I, Chapter 6, page 69) is reached. At this stage, the *natural weapons* function as if they had a **MIND** of their own. The thinking process is governed by *subconscious reaction* which takes full reign of the body. The *conscious* mind, it seems, has no function. *Conscious* thoughts and feelings do not hinder the immediate task of defending or attacking. Strategies and plans of defense and offense are not thought of *consciously*--they just naturally happen. If the attack is real, so is the response. Properly trained **MENTALLY** and **PHYSICALLY**, the body and mind automatically responds to any given situation.

The following are descriptions and illustrations of the most useful exercises:

WARM-UP EXERCISES

The following exercises should be used to loosen and limber the body prior to doing your strengthening exercises.

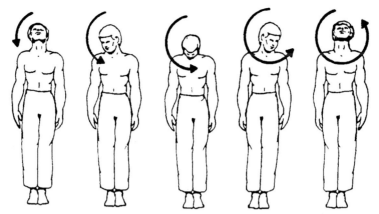

I-3 HEAD ROTATIONS -- to loosen and limber the neck.

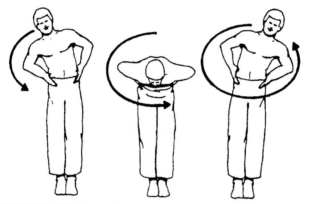

I-4 HIP ROTATIONS -- to loosen and limber the hips and waist.

I-5 SIDE BENDS -- another exercise to loosen the hips and waist.

23

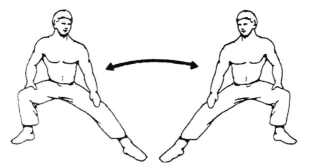

I-6   LEG STRETCHES -- to loosen the thighs and calf.

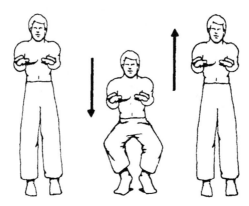

I-7   LEG SQUATS -- to limber the thighs and calf.

STRENGTHENING EXERCISES

Please start the following strengthening exercises moderately before increasing the number of repetitions.

I-8   PUSH UPS—using the finger tips.
Starting Position: Facing floor, body straight from head to heels, weight supported on fingers and toes.

Movement:

(1) Keeping body straight, bend elbows and touch chest to ground.

(2) Straighten elbows and return to starting position

(3) Do three (3) sets of five (5) repetitions. Increase repetitions when able.

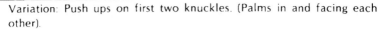

Variation: Push ups on first two knuckles. (Palms in and facing each other).

I-9 PUSH UPS—a variation for developing the triceps.

Starting Position: Facing floor, body straight from head to heels, weight supported on forearms and toes. Hands overlap, elbows twelve to eighteen inches apart so that a triangle is formed.

Movement:

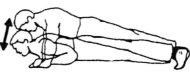

(1) Keeping body straight, push and straighten elbows, using tricep strength only.

(2) Bend elbows and return to starting position, touching head to hands.

(3) Do three (3) sets of fifteen (15) repetitions.

Variation: Lower chest to hands.

NOTE: Place feet on chair for added resistance.

I-10 PUSH AWAYS—to strengthen the fingers and wrists.

Starting Position: Facing wall, body straight from head to heels, weight supported on hands and feet. Hands placed at eye level, feet about two (2) feet from wall.

Movement:

(1) Keeping body and arms straight, push body away from wall until weight is on fingertips.

(2) Return to starting position.

(3) Do three (3) sets of ten (10) repetitions when strength increases. Also, as strength increases support weight with fewer fingers; that is, four fingers, then three, etc.

NOTE: To increase resistance, move feet back as you move hands down.

I-11 PULLUPS—requires a horizontal bar and is used to develop biceps.

Starting Position: Hanging at full length from the bar; with arms straight, grasp the bar with hands wide apart and with a reverse grip.

Movement:

(1) Pull up until the chin is above the bar.

(2) Lower the body until elbows are completely straight.

(3) Do as many repetitions as possible.

25

I-12 LEG RAISES—for developing the stomach (abdominals).

Starting Position: On back, arms to the side, palms down, legs straight.

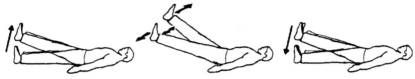

Movement:

    (1)   Raise legs six (6) inches above the floor.

    (2)   Spread legs wide.

    (3)   Close legs again.

    (4)   Lower legs to starting position.

    (5)   Do two (2) sets of twenty-five (25) to fifty (50) repetitions.

I-13 V-UPS—for developing the stomach (abdominals).

Starting Position: On back, arms to the side, palms down, legs straight. Inhale before executing first movement.

Movement:

    (1)   Raise legs with knees straight. Simultaneously sit up and touch the toes with the fingers, keeping arms straight. Have trunk and legs form a V position. Exhale as you touch toes.

    (2)   Return to starting position. Inhale on way down.

    (3)   Do three (3) sets of twenty (20) repetitions.

I-14 SITUPS—using an abdominal board elevated from a 35 to 40 degree angle to the floor (for developing the stomach—abdominals).

Starting Position: On back, hands tucked under head, legs straight and ankles strapped at the higher end of the board. Inhale before executing first movement.

Movement:

    (1)   Sit up as far forward as possible; exhale on the way up.

    (2)   Return to starting position. Inhale on way down.

    (3)   Do three (3) sets of twenty (20) repetitions.

I-15 BACK RAISES—using a table to strengthen the lower back.

Starting Position: Lying on table face down, with upper torso extending over edge of table at the waist, bend as far over as possible. Hands clasped behind head, ankles pinned or strapped to table. Inhale before executing first movement.

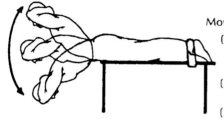

Movement:

    (1) Raise upper torso as far back as possible. Exhale on way down.

    (2) Return to starting position. Inhale on way down.

    (3) Do three (3) sets of twenty (20) repetitions.

I-16 SIDE LEG RAISES—for strengthening the hips and loins.

Starting Position: Standing erect with feet together, forearms horizontally raised, elbows resting against ribs.

Movement

    (1) Slowly raise left leg directly to the side and as high as possible.

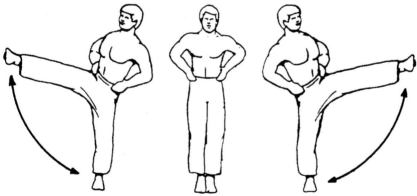

    (2) Return to starting position.

    (3) Slowly raise right leg directly to the side and as high as possible.

    (4) Return to starting position.

    (5) Do two (2) sets of ten (10) repetitions with each leg.

NOTE: For added resistance wear heavy boots or attach iron boots to feet.

I-17   STANDING JUMPS — to develop the hips and loins.

Starting Position: Standing erect with feet flat and together, arms placed smartly to the side.

Movement:

(1)   Jump straight up. At greatest height, tuck legs in, raise them to chest and have arms embrace legs. Try to jump as high as possible each time.

(2)   Return to starting position.

(3)   Do two (2) sets of ten (10) repetitions.

I-18   SQUAT JUMPS — to develop the thighs, calves and ankles.

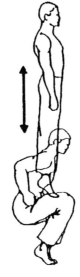

Starting Position: Standing erect with feet flat and together, arms placed smartly to the side.

Movement:

(1)   Squat low on toes.

(2)   Leap as high as possible.

(3)   Return to squatting position.

(4)   Do two (2) sets of twenty (20) repetitions.

Variation: Do squats flat footed. Light dumbells can be held at the sides of the hips with each jump.

I-19 RAISE ON TOES—using two by four board to strengthen calves and ankles.

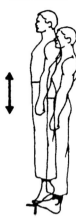

Starting Position: Place toes on two by four, arms placed smartly to the sides. Keep knees straight throughout exercise.

Movement:

   (1)   Raise up on toes as high as possible.

   (2)   Slowly return to starting position.

   (3)   Do two (2) sets of twenty (20) to thirty (30) repetitions.

Variations: Point toes either straight, in, or out. Use weights as strength increases.

CHAPTER 4
BASICS

Technically speaking, **BASICS** are all physical moves or gestures executed with specific intent or purpose. Depending upon how these moves or gestures are employed, they can be defensive, offensive, or can accomplish both purposes simultaneously. When applied, they can be used to oppose, ride, borrow, or steal force, faint, sprain, dislocate, fracture, rupture, maim, rip, tear, claw, hook, poke, slice, rake, buckle, check, maneuver, trip, grab, lock, twist, pinch, butt, bite, throw, pull, along with numerous other accomplishments.

As already established, each **BASIC** move literally constitutes an alphabet of motion and when combined to form words, sentences, and paragraphs of motion, they *can* accomplish the stated effects.

The importance of **BASICS** can never be over emphasized. Each **BASIC** move learned must be performed with continual precision. Here, as in grammar school, we must learn each move, or alphabet of motion, phonetically. While learning to formulate words of motion, we must employ physical pronunciation, enunciation, and diction so that each move used rapidly within a combination sequence, becomes distinct, not muddled, in its application. Poorly learned or weak **BASICS** can literally cause you to "mumble" with your movements. "Mumbling motion" is like mumbling words, they are meaningless and serve no real or useful purpose except to display your own frustration.

The method used in teaching moves via phonetics is one that has been employed by many who are involved with body motion. Each move is broken down into numbered stages. As each move is taught *by-the-numbers,* correct hand or foot positions are stressed. Position changes of the hands and feet continue with each numbered move so that the student learns the value of torque, complete utilization of body weight, and all other ingredients necessary to complete and/or maximize the move. (For it must again be emphasized that **BASIC** moves or gestures in and of themselves are not complete in maximizing your efforts.)

Although the *by-the-number* method is an ideal way to learn moves phonetically, it is not to be used in a realistic situation. This *by-the-number* method is an exercise in slow motion that freezes with each count. Once phonetics are learned and maximum power is experienced with each move (if and when needed) numbered stages are eliminated and condensation of motion without the loss of maximum power takes precedent. Just as we do not speak to each other phonetically on a daily basis; likewise, phonetics of motion are also dropped during the course of higher learning and/or actual combat.

This *by-the-number* method is highly recommended, but once you have learned each move from an idealistic standpoint, be sure to condense each move without losing the same power impact. Remember, physical phonetics can only benefit you if you can train your body to execute maximum force via conserved motion. Once this is learned, motion can be conserved in three ways. First, movements become direct, that is, *by-the-number* cocking or winding up motion is eliminated. For example, the fist does not draw back to gain greater blocking or striking distance and power--it goes from its point of origin. Second, at the advanced stage, the *"ands"* are eliminated from the response. Instead of blocking *"and"* hurting, or grabbing *"and"* hurting, the defense and offense occurs simultaneously. Third, by combining several strikes into one basic motion, combinations are executed at faster speeds. For example, the fingers can be directed to the eyes after a chop to the neck, or an elbow can follow right behind the action of the fist.

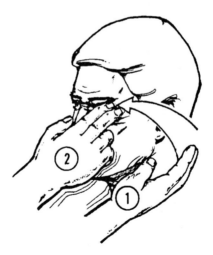

I-20 After a (1) chop to the neck, the fingers can be (2) directed to the eyes by slicing or hooking.

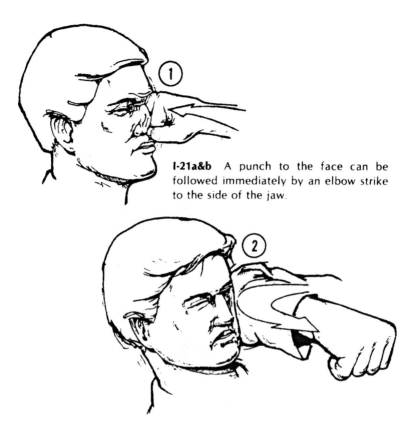

I-21a&b A punch to the face can be followed immediately by an elbow strike to the side of the jaw.

Visual aids are also needed while teaching **BASICS**. These aids can be of two varieties--tangible or intangible. Tangible visual aids refer to actual objects, photos, illustrated drawings, or demonstrated moves, used to put a point across that can be seen or felt. Intangible visual aids are mental pictures implanted in the minds of the practitioner which either follow a specific angle, direction, or path with his arms or legs. Although the point stressed cannot be seen by the naked eye, it can be seen by the inner eye--the mind.

I use a number of visual aids (tangible as well as intangible) to make learning easier. To help a student visualize an accurate direction, I use what I term the *"clock principle"*. This is a mental visual aid used to teach a student the proper positioning of his feet in the performance of his **BASICS**, self-defense techniques, freestyle techniques, forms (katas), etc. For example, before starting a form (kata), a student should picture himself standing in the middle of a large clock that has been placed on the floor (see illustration on next page). The wall he faces should represent 12 o'clock, to his right, 3 o'clock, directly behind of him, 6 o'clock, and to his left, 9 o'clock. As he moves from his starting position, having a knowledge of where other points on the clock are will help him perform his moves with a more definite sense of direction. This principle also applies while learning self-defense techniques. 12 o'clock will always be the starting direction he faces regardless of where the attack stems -- flank, rear, or otherwise. Let me present another situation, the student may be facing 12 o'clock with his opponent attacking from 3 o'clock and be asked to have his left foot step back to 9 o'clock as he faces his opponent attacking from 3 o'clock. Three facets were involved here -- the original direction in which he was facing (12 o'clock), the angle from which his opponent attacked him (3 o'clock), and the correct position of his foot (9 o'clock) which is necessary to thwart the attack.

In short, the "clock principle" is a directional reference used to aid a student in selecting the proper direction when attacked, retaliating, or working his BASICS.

I-22 The "clock principle" suggests that a student picture himself standing in the middle of a large clock facing 12 o'clock.

To further simplify my teaching methods, so that students can readily understand and retain what is taught, I employ what I term the "mathematic and geometric symbol concepts". These are visual aids that can be used tangibly or intangibly. As stated, this can be accomplished by using actual illustrations so that a student can see it, or through verbalizing a mental picture instead.

There are three (3) mathematic and three (3) geometric symbols that can enhance student learning. The three mathematic symbols are the minus sign (-) used in subtraction, the plus sign (+) used in addition, and the times sign (x) used in multiplication. To elaborate (this method of analyzation should be adopted and used continuously in your learning process), a plus sign (+) is no more than two minus signs, one horizontal (-) the other vertical (|) that is superimposed with one over the other. Upon examining the multiplication sign (x), it can be said that it is no more than a plus sign (+) which has fallen on its side (x). The three (3) geometric symbols are the square (□), triangle (△), and the circle (O). Analyzation will help you to deduct that a triangle is no more than half a square (◩) that has slipped from the original structure. All of these symbols will be used periodically throughout the text to simplify your learning.

The "mathematic and geometric symbol concepts" can be paralleled with the "clock principle" and, therefore, both methods can be used interchangeably -- thus providing similar results and benefits. For example, a line drawn from 9 o'clock to 3 o'clock will give you a minus sign (-), superimpose it with a line from 12 o'clock to 6 o'clock and it will create a plus sign (+). Draw a straight line from 8 to 2 and superimpose a straight line from 10 to 4, and you will have a multiplication sign (x). Connect all of the numbers with an arc and you will come up with a circle (O) -- see illustration. Draw straight lines as shown in illustration I23b and you will develop a square (□), divide your square as shown in illustration I23c and you will come up with a traingle (△).

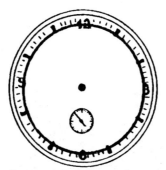

I-23a Connect all of the numbers with an arc and you will have a circle.

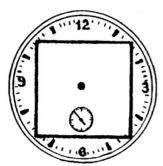

I-23b Draw four lines within the clock's circumference and you will develop a square.

I-23c Divide the square in half within the circle and you will have formed two triangles.

Another value that the clock, mathematic, and geometric concepts offer (other than aiding you in determining proper angles and directions), is the help it gives you in proportionately fitting the Art to the specific measurements of an individual. Through its use, a student can obtain the proper *width, depth,* and *height* (as it relates to his body size) of a specific stance; or he may be able to use it to control the *width, depth,* and *height* zones of an attacking opponent. These concepts will be elaborated upon in Chapter 6.

A more sophisticated visual aid encompassing all of these methods, plus additional ones can be found in the *"Universal Pattern"* (see illustration). I conceived this pattern while reviewing training films of myself in reverse during my early years of training (refer to Volume IV, Chapter 8). Viewing my movements in reverse, a dimension I had not even considered was revealed. I instantly realized how limited I was in my observation of movements. I had been aware of only half of the value contained within my moves--the other half had remained hidden. How or why this revelation even came to me I do not know, but I do know, that since that time, untold avenues have opened up and thus given me a more thorough understanding of the Martial Arts. Because of this added knowledge, I have learned how to change embryonic moves to sophisticated moves, to differentiate between the terms opposite and reverse, and how reversing action can be applied defensively or offensively within the *"double factor"* concept.

I-24 The Universal Pattern -- a useful devise to study and understand the theories of motion.

The *"Universal Pattern"*, as shown, is only one fifth (1/5) complete; however, contained within this diagram are sufficient answers for this text. Utilizing this pattern, you will learn to apply it to your activities in the Martial Arts. A detailed explanation of the *"Universal Pattern"* in its entirety would take several volumes to write. Explanations found in Volume IV, Chapter 8, should suffice.

I am convinced that **BASICS** can be more thoroughly understood, of greater value, and more quickly learned if the teaching method employed comparative analysis of everyday occurrences. When a student can relate to something or some concept that he is already familiar with, **BASICS** become easier to learn. His having experienced the concept in another field (related or not), eases substitution of his newly learned skill. Therefore, when this new experience and/or concept parallels his old, he can be assured that he is getting closer to understanding this new concept.

Another unique teaching technique, which I often employ while teaching **BASICS**, is what I term the *"rearrangement concept"*. This teaching concept helps a new student to realize how *limited knowledge* can be *expanded upon.* Since many, who study the Martial Arts, are not interested in becoming professional Martial Artists and are only interested in obtaining sufficient knowledge of how to cope with average encounters, the *"rearrangement concept"* works well. For example, it teaches you how four (4) **BASIC** moves, through rearranging, can produce twenty-four (24) possible combinations without using the same combination twice. Why is this important? What significance or bearing does this have to the Martial Arts? The answer rests in the term *"sophisticated simplicity"*. If a student has mastered four moves with a complete knowledge of the twenty-four ways they can be rearranged, and can apply them extemporaneously and effectively, he is far ahead of the student who knows twenty-four moves well, but has *no* knowledge of the *"rearrangement concept"*.

Knowledge of the *"rearrangement concept"* is important because there are no two situations exactly alike in a confrontation. Therefore, to have a set sequence of moves in mind when countering your opponent is unrealistic. With a thorough knowledge of the *"rearrangement concept"*, you are capable of blending with the action as it occurs even though your knowledge of moves may be limited. It is the expansion of your limited knowledge that will give you the edge.

There are two *"rearrangement concepts"*--the *"numerical"* and the *"alphabetical"*.

Here is how the "numerical rearrangement concept" works. If you have knowledge of four moves, give each move a number. Now that you have numbers associated with each move, the formula in determining how many combinations there are, without repeating yourself, can be found as follows: $1 \times 2 = 2$, $2 \times 3 = 6$, and $6 \times 4 = 24$. If you wanted to determine the number of combinations that five moves would produce, etc., then multiply 5×24, which will give you an answer of 120, $6 \times 120 = 720$, $7 \times 720 = 5,040$, etc. (Please refer to page 37 to see how this concept is applied.)

The "alphabetical rearrangement concept" follows the same format used in the formation of words. Letters picked from our alphabetic system, when properly arranged, can create words that are familiar to us. Like the "numerical rearrangement concept", limited knowledge of the complete alphabetic system can still prove effective if the "rearrangement concept" is thoroughly understood. A student who only learns the alphabet from A to G can still benefit from his limited knowledge provided he learns that from these seven letters of the alphabet, he can create words such as AD, DAB, ACE, FACE, FED, FAD, DEAF, etc. When each of these seven letters of the alphabet are used more than once, words such as DEED, DAD, etc. can then be created. Since each move learned can be considered an *alphabet of motion,* we can create a surprisingly large number of *words of motion* even though our knowledge of the *alphabets of motion* may be limited. (See Volume V for further elaboration.) Therefore, if a student studied the Martial Arts for a short time, left for a period of time, and then resumed his training, his newly acquired knowledge of *alphabets of motion* combined with his previously mastered **BASICS**, would greatly expand his *vocabulary of motion.* As already mentioned, this would only occur if the "alphabetical rearrangement concept" was thoroughly mastered. Every effort should therefore be made to master your "rearrangement concepts" of **BASICS**.

Make every effort to utilize **BASICS** using the aforementioned methods. Learning correct **BASIC** movements, as described, will aid you in converting embryonic movements to sophisticated movements. In simpler terms, perfected **BASICS** will automatically convert crude or embryonic moves to polished or sophisticated ones. As these moves become automatic in their application and execution, you will discover, as I have, that the Martial Arts are not complicated but sophisticated. And what is sophistication? No more than simple compounded **BASIC** moves--one move added upon another, etc. Thus, you will further discover that the limit of Martial Art knowledge should ideally border on the outer realm of simplicity and the starting point of what seems complex but really isn't.

Obviously there are many approaches to teaching **BASICS**. Whatever the approach, I admonish you to follow a progressive lesson plan geared to individual ability. Determine your strong points as well as those that come naturally, then proceed to cultivate these positive attributes first. When an individual learns what he can do naturally, he can then apply what he has learned the very day he is taught.

As a reminder--do not discard, but store simple movements that are replaced by those of sophistication. Avoid the temptation to discard your basic knowledge because of newly acquired and improved skills.

To best understand what a "numerical rearrangement" concept involves, let us examine a self-defense technique containing four moves and assign each move a number from one (1) to four (4). Assuming that the sequence of four moves flows without interruption, let us assign number one (1) to a right inward block executed on the inside of your opponent's right punch; number two (2) to a right chop executed at the right side of your opponent's neck; number three (3) to a right inward horizontal elbow strike to the right side of your opponent's jaw; and number four (4) to a right back downward hammerfist strike to your opponent's groin. This sequential flow of movements can be extremely effective if your opponent responds to your action and makes no effort to intentionally or unintentionally obstruct your flow of four sequential movements.

FP-1 When your opponent throws a right punch, step to the inside of his punch as you execute a right inward block to the inside of his right forearm. Make sure that your left hand is placed in a defensive position.

FP-2 As your right hand converts into a chop, strike to the right side of your opponent's neck as you simultaneously check your opponent's right arm with your left hand.

FP-3 Do a Push Drag shuffle as you simultaneously execute a right horizontal inward elbow strike to the left side of your opponent's jaw with a left heel plam strike to the opposite jaw to cause a sandwiching effect.

FP-4 Pivot couterclockwise as you remain inplace and execute a right downward back hammerfist strike to your opponent's groin as you shift your left hand to a high guarding position.

Now let us assume that an opponent does make an effort to defend himself by placing his left hand in a guarding postion. If this occurs, let us now see how we can still use the same four moves by execersing a simple sequencial change employing the "numerical rearrangement" concept to make it work. Although the sequence of movements will be altered an uninterrupted flow can still be obtained inspite of your opponent's attempt to protect himself.

FP-5 The first move is the same as FP-1 with one exception, your opponent's left hand is in a guarding position.

FP-6 From the originally FP-1, shift into what was FP-4.

FP-7 Now execute what was FP-3.

FP-8 Conclude with what was Fp-2.

CHAPTER 5
DIVISIONS OF THE BASICS

BASICS are divided into five major divisions--**STANCES, MANEUVERS, BLOCKS, STRIKES,** and **SPECIALIZED MOVES** and **METHODS** (moves and methods unrelated to the first four divisions that have distinct characteristics of their own). When **BASICS** from each division are employed, they may be used independently within their division, combined with those of another division, or combined with **BASICS** from all divisions.

The name for each **BASIC** move is often developed from three sources--method of execution, specific part of the anatomy used in the execution, or the final position after execution. For example, if a **BLOCK** is delivered outside of your body structure and then *in* and toward it, it is considered an **INWARD BLOCK.** If the **BLOCK** is delivered inside of your body structure and then *out* and away from it, it is considered an **OUTWARD BLOCK.** If it is delivered *up* and above your body structure, is is considered an **UPWARD BLOCK,** and if *down* and below, a **DOWNWARD BLOCK.** A **KNIFE-EDGE CHOP** would be a descriptive term used for a specific part of the hand (anatomy) used in executing the **CHOP.** In using a **STANCE,** the final position may resemble a rider on a horse--thus the term "HORSE STANCE" is given to this **STANCE.**

Each **BASIC** division is further divided into subdivisions. Please refer to the Chapters corresponding to each of the five major divisions for detailed explanation.

In summation, it can be said of **BASICS** that of the first four major divisions, **STANCES** are literally *postures* of defense and offense, **MANEUVERS** are *methods of travel, and/or body positioning* to enhance defense or offense. **BLOCKS** are *methods of defense,* and **STRIKES** are *methods of offense.* The fifth division identifies those moves and methods that cannot be categorized under the first four divisions and that unquestionably contain individual characteristics of their own. **SPECIALIZED MOVES AND METHODS** can be used defensively and offensively.

Please review the following *charts* thoroughly. Studying them will give you a more comprehensive knowledge of the anatomical breakdown of the **BASICS** of the Martial Arts and how they relate to one another.

ORGANIZATIONAL CHART ON BASICS

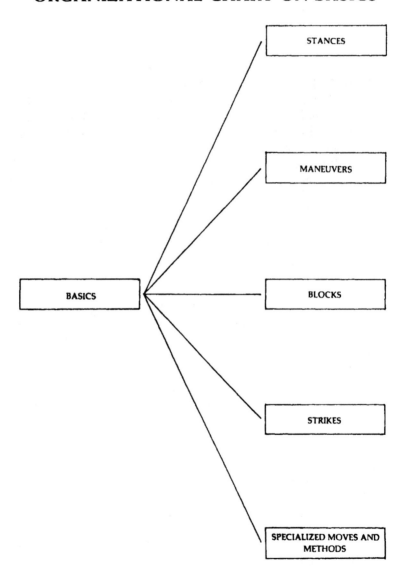

BASICS

STANCES

MANEUVERS

BLOCKS

STRIKES

SPECIALIZED MOVES AND METHODS

CHAPTER 6
STANCES

STANCES are important because they form the foundation of all self-defense moves. Although they may seem unnatural at first, they are not difficult to master. Mastery comes through repetition and practice--a must in overcoming obstacles and insuring progress.

STANCE development often involves strengthening and limbering the leg muscles. (In fact, it is not uncommon, at first, for the legs to burn with fatigue.) Ultimately each STANCE will develop to the point where the legs can relax and yet still maintain the correct positioning (form). However, the most important method in which to develop each STANCE, is to perfect them in *motion* and not in a stationary state. Through such development, STANCE changes become effortless, your speed, poise and balance will be enhanced, and spring action will be available instantaneously.

The most noticeable aspect of STANCES in motion, although not absolute, is the proud erect posture which allows a practitioner to flow across the ground. Even when kicking or maneuvering, the practitioner's erect posture and calm expression do not betray him.

Although many of the STANCES described on the following pages appear to be contrary to conventional methods, there are valid reasons for doing them. Conventional methods are primarily concerned with strikes which are executed *above the waistline.* STANCES described in this text are in anticipation of natural weapons which may be delivered *below, as well as above, the waistline.* STANCE consideration should also encompass the possibility of multiple attacks.

Many benefits can be derived from STANCES. They improve balance, give automatic protection to vulnerable areas, can be used to increase or decrease distance, aid in increasing one's power, assist in buckling, checking or breaking an opponent's leg, allows for greater maneuverability, enhances an individual's peripheral vision and much more.

STANCES can be learned in a variety of ways. *Stationary* STANCES are used when you are practicing movements of the upper body in order to minimize confusion. The movements of the upper body alone can be extremely taxing during the initial stages of learning. To include coordinated moves with the lower half of the body too soon would only be frustrating and discouraging. Simplicity and repetition are the keys to ultimate proficiency.

From *stationary* **STANCES**, you progress to **STANCE** *changes while in place.* This phase of training incorporates shifting your weight to (1) increase range, or to (2) decrease existing range. When the first benefit is achieved, distance becomes your ally. Generally, the desired distance is determined by the position of the upper portion of the body.

When employing *in place* **STANCE** changes, you do not have to move your feet to change into a different **STANCE.** You merely shift your weight to change your **STANCE**--which is an accomplishment in itself. This significantly reduces time and contributes to economy of motion (see illustration I-26). Futhermore, by remaining in place, your ability to couter attack is greatly enhanced because unnecessary steps have been eliminated.

I-26 This illustration depicts an in-place stance change from (1) a right Neutral Bow Stance where the weight distribution is 50-50 on either leg. You can (2) shift into a right Reverse Bow, where the weight distribution is 40% on the right leg and 60% on the left leg. As you can observe, sufficient distance can be achieved by simply shifting your stance and re-distributing your body weight. In doing so, you will automatically make distance your ally.

Several beneficial by-products are achieved when you decrease your range. Primarily it increases power. Second, it aids in increasing the speed of your actions. Third, it allows you to crowd your opponent, making it possible for you to check his actions. In other words, there are two ways to avoid being hit: (1) create enough distance between you and your opponent, or (2) crowd and muffle your opponent's moves so that he is greatly limited in what he can do. This second method is reserved for the more proficient student and is not recommended for the beginner.

The third method of learning **STANCES** is practicing **STANCES** *in motion*. There are many ways to accomplish this. Depending upon what you wish to accomplish and as circumstances dictate, you can walk, cross over, cross back, slide, shuffle, hop, skip, jump, or leap with them. When combining these methods, **STANCES** can be lost in transition. However, if you were to isolate each move, specific **STANCES** are distinguishable. In other words, within a sequence of **STANCE** *changes in motion, transitory* **STANCES** occur. These are **STANCES** that are not intended to be held for any length of time, but, nevertheless, help the flow of motion.

Through continuous practice, you will execute **STANCE** *changes in motion* with balance, poise, and power. Ultimately, you will also learn to relax, maintain correct form, and move with effortless speed. **STANCES** *in motion* can also be classified as **FOOT MANEUVERS** (see Chapter 7 on **MANEUVERS** on page 105).

Each **STANCE** must be taught to suit the individual. The width, depth, and height of each **STANCE** varies with each individual. Ways of discovering the proper width, depth and height of each **STANCE** will be described and illustrated in this text (see pages   to   ). Study these methods thoroughly. They will aid you in making each **STANCE** work more effectively for you.

All Art forms employ similar principles. It is when you take the time to analyze and compare them that these truths become apparent. As mentioned, **STANCES** should be tailored to the individual. The height, width, and depth of a **STANCE** should be arrived at according to the size, weight, and height of the individual. This concept can be compared with Piccaso, Rembrandt, and Michael Angelo paintings. They were all famous artists whose paintings varied in style, but their artistic works were *constant* in the illusion of height, width, and depth. If these *dimensional principles* apply among great artists, is it not logical that these same principles should be applied to the Martial Arts? *Dimensional principles* keep all art forms in perspective.

Hand and body positions along with **STANCES** are also important to learn. While maneuvering, a change of *hand and body positions* should be coordinated with each **STANCE** *change*. While a particular **STANCE** allows better protection for the lower region of the body, the fact remains that the hands and body should also be positioned in preparation for an unanticipated strike, a premeditated attack, or a counter attack. The coordination of *hand positions, body positions* and **STANCE WORK** cannot be minimized. It is of utmost importance that they are used simultaneously. This aspect will be illustrated periodically throughout the text along with the concept of **CHECKING** .

47

ORGANIZATIONAL CHART ON STANCES

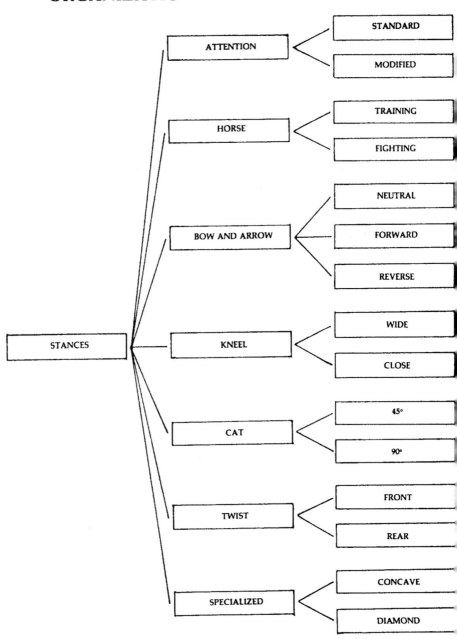

ATTENTION STANCE

ATTENTION STANCE - This **STANCE** is used when conveying instructional information to the students. It is also used as an interim **STANCE** prior to giving a command. When a command is given, the student will react from the **ATTENTION STANCE**. Other than these uses, its value in combat is extremely limited. Regardless of its limitations, it can be useful during class instructions and also during rare occasions in combat. In addition, it can also be considered a disciplining **STANCE**.

Its name originated from the fact that it is almost identical to the *attention position* found in most branches of the Military (see illustrations below). Here, as in the Military and other similar agencies, the feet are placed together with both feet flat, the weight equally distributed between both feet, the head erect, and the back straight.

This **STANCE** does not require adjustment to find the dimensions related to you. It is simple and requires no further explanation other than what has been stated.

ANALYTICAL STUDY
OF THE ATTENTION STANCE

FRONT VIEW　　　　　　　**SIDE VIEW**

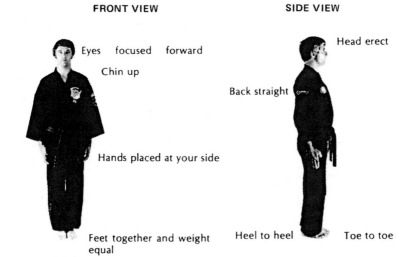

Eyes focused forward

Chin up

Hands placed at your side

Feet together and weight equal

Head erect

Back straight

Heel to heel　　Toe to toe

49

DATA SUMMATION
OF THE ATTENTION STANCE

Foot Position: Feet together - Toe-Toe / Heel-Heel

Weight Distribution: 50-50

Reason and Purpose: To convey instructional information, to teach discipline and respect, and help you to be more attentive.

Explanation: With your feet together, have both of your arms hang parallel to your trousers, with your palms facing your legs. Keep your head and back erect with your eyes focused straight ahead. You then await commands from this stance.

HORSE STANCE

HORSE STANCE - This STANCE literally replaces standing up. The HORSE STANCES are of two types--the *TRAINING* HORSE and the *FIGHTING* HORSE. At all KENPO schools, the *TRAINING* HORSE is the basic exercise position for learning blocks, punches, kicks, etc. and for warming up. (It is also used as a ritual when beginning and closing classes at all of my schools.) From it, the student develops erect posture, balance, and power--which is generated from a solid (stationary) STANCE. The HORSE STANCE is also frequently used in forms, self-defense techniques, and free-style techniques as an important STANCE change. However, the *NEUTRAL* BOW AND ARROW STANCE (see page 60) is a more versatile STANCE for sparring.

The HORSE STANCE (illustration I-29) gets its name from the fact that it resembles the position used while riding a horse (see page 54). It is bilaterally symmetrical—that is, the right half looks exactly like the left half (see photo). The weight is equally distributed between both feet which are flat and slightly pigeon toed. If you will notice in the photo, the back is straight and the rump tucked in.

The correct method to obtain a HORSE STANCE is to bend the knees slightly forward and force them out to the sides as though they were being pushed apart (which can be achieved with practice). The feet must be held in place. Avoid bending the knees too far forward or placing the feet too far apart.

The distance between feet is critical, but it will vary according to the size of the individual (generally slightly over shoulder width apart). Study the illustrated photos and try to develop the *width* and *height* of the *TRAINING* **HORSE** suited to your proportions. In finding the dimensions of the *FIGHTING* **HORSE**, *depth* and *height* are the only two considerations. Keep in mind that if the feet are too close together, the **STANCE** is weakened and balance poor. Likewise, if they are too far apart, **STANCE** changes and kicking become difficult and maneuverability hampered.

The *FIGHTING* **HORSE** (see photos on page 53) is almost identical to the *TRAINING* **HORSE**. The difference lies in placing your feet in the direction you are facing. Thus, both feet are in line with your direction of focus. See illustration on page 52 .

ANALYTICAL STUDY
OF THE HORSE STANCES

Training Horse

FRONT VIEW

Keep your chin up.

Relax your shoulders.

Keep your head erect and body perpendicular to the ground (floor).

Force your knees out and away from you.

Place greater stress on the outer portion of your calf muscles.

Your feet should be slightly wider than the width of your shoulders. Once the proper width has been determined, bend both of your knees naturally and comfortably and you will automatically find your proper height.

TOP VIEW

Your shoulders parallel your hips.

Your body weight is equally distributed between both legs.

Notice the use of plus (+) sign.

Your feet are pigeon toed. (If you were to extend two imaginary lines in the direction your toes are pointed, both lines would intersect at a given point.)

SIDE VIEW

Your eyes should be focused straight ahead.

Your back must be straight.

Force your chest out slightly.

Your buttocks should be tucked in and your weight dropped so as to aid you in lowering your center of gravity.

Keep your knees bent and have your knee caps directly over the ends of your toes.

Your feet should be flat and should literally grip the ground.

Fighting Horse

Facing your opponent sideways (to the flank) is what makes the *Fighting Horse* differ from the *Training Horse*.

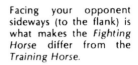

Keep your rear arm down to protect the middle region of your body.

Keep your forward arm up to protect the upper region of your body.

Your feet should be pigeon toed. Both feet should be placed on your line of sight with one directly behind the other.

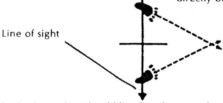

Line of sight

Although both of your feet should be placed on your line of sight, extended lines pointing in the direction of the toes should also intersect at a given point.

SIDE VIEW

Focus your attention toward the direction of your lead. leg. (If your right foot is forward, look to your right, if your left foot is forward, look to your left.)

Notice the use of a minus (-) sign.

Line of sight

AN INTERESTING COMPARISON

The knee can be compared with a shock absorber and should, therefore, be thought of as one. It should remain flexible between moves, remaining stable when and where necessary, and subject to instant directional change.

I-28   The knee should be compared to a shock absorber.

HOW THE HORSE STANCE GOT ITS NAME

I-29   The Horse Stance resembles a person in a seated position riding a horse.

FINDING THE PROPER DIMENSIONS

As I have previously stressed and will continue to stress, the Art must be made to fit the individual in order to produce maximum, as well as, positive results. Therefore, the *width, depth* and *height* of a **STANCE** must correspond with the dimensions of the individual. To give specific measurements to any of the **STANCES** (for example to say that there should be exactly 12 inches between your feet, etc.) is absurd. The length and size of a leg or foot must be considered and compensated for so that adjustments can be correctly made.

The *TRAINING* **HORSE** involves *height* and *width* only--the *FIGHTING* **HORSE,** dimensions of *height* and *depth.* The following methods can be used to correctly determine dimensions related to you.

P-14a-d (a) Place both feet together; (b) turn both heels out; (c) turn the toes of both feet out; and (d) conclude by comfortably turning both heels out again. This is one of the methods of proportionately finding the correct Horse Stance for you.

The method just described should aid you in finding the correct *width* of your *TRAINING* **HORSE STANCE.** Once determining your *width,* squat comfortably and you will automatically obtain the proper *height.* In time, a step to your right or left (see illustrations on page **56**) will be sufficient to find the proper *width* of your *TRAINING* **HORSE STANCE.** Experience and time will make consistence habitual.

(2a)

(1)

(2b)

Step to your right   With feet together   Step to your left

The following method will aid you in determining the proper dimensions for a *FIGHTING* **HORSE STANCE.**

(1) Place a line on the ground that will represent your line of sight.

(2) Now plant both feet on your line of sight so that your feet and body are parallel with the line.

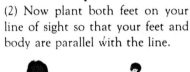

(3) Execute and form a *Training Horse Stance* on your line of sight. Follow the same procedure as described on page 55 in determining the proper width.

(4) At this stage, turn your head and focus your eyes in the same direction as your line of sight (as if looking to the flank).

In summation, the *FIGHTING* **HORSE** basically has no *width*. However, to establish the proper *depth* of your *FIGHTING* **HORSE,** you must first find the *width* of your *TRAINING* **HORSE** on your line of sight. After this position has been established, have your head and eyes turn in the direction of your line of sight. By doing so, you will automatically obtain the desired *depth* of your *FIGHTING* **HORSE.** When your *depth* is ascertained, have both of your knees bend comfortably to establish the correct *height.*

If you still question the importance of proper dimensions as they relate to you, remember they unquestionably aid you in functioning more effectively and efficiently. They incorporate those added ingredients necessary to achieve superiority. You can do without them, but with them, your skill will be unmatched.

AN ADDED HELP

The following method has been used for centuries to correct the *width* of a student's **HORSE STANCE**. As your knees are forced out, they should bow out so that the sides of your calf muscles protrude slightly beyond the *width* of your ankles. This angling will prevent a foot stomp injury that may originate from the top and side of your calf muscle down and to your foot. The following illustrations should be an aid in clarifying this point.

Place the knife-edge of your foot at the top of your partner's calf (at knee level).

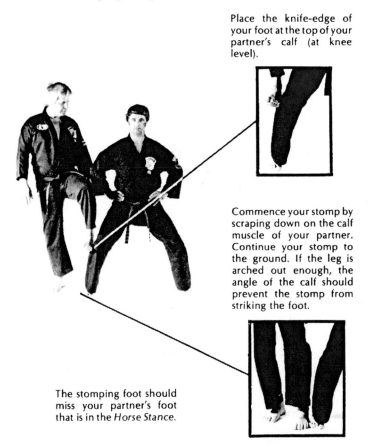

Commence your stomp by scraping down on the calf muscle of your partner. Continue your stomp to the ground. If the leg is arched out enough, the angle of the calf should prevent the stomp from striking the foot.

The stomping foot should miss your partner's foot that is in the *Horse Stance*.

HISTORICAL INTEREST

It is logical that innovations will develop with time. Environmental changes dictate this fact. However, it is often interesting to learn what others did throughout history as well as how they thought. Granted, in most instances, methods used in the past would perhaps not apply today; nevertheless, the *why* and *how* they developed has always intrigued me.

Because of the restrictive attire worn by monks in the monastaries of China, they first kicked their leg into the air before planting that foot into a **HORSE STANCE**. This move was executed in the shape of an arc traveling from *inside out*. It was expedient during that period of history to reach the bottom of their robes so that they could quickly gather and tuck the end under their belt. This action prepared them for combat. (See illustrations below). Executing this maneuver enabled them to move about more freely. Tripping, stumbling or other hazardous encumbrances were minimized if not eliminated.

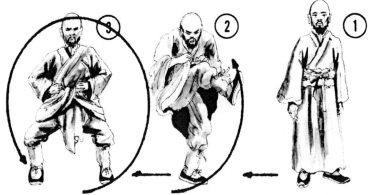

I-31a-c The above illustrations depict one of the methods used by Chinese monks to gather and tuck their robes under or over their belts or sashes as they prepared themselves for combat.

Traditional forms (classical katas) or sets are still executed in this manner today. They are beautiful to see and preserve their esthetic value. The only setback is that they are being done without purpose (in some cases). It is important that we know the meaning for each move so that we can make the distinction between what is traditional, and most important, whether it is practical or impractical. It must be emphasized, however, that while modern clothing eliminates the practicality of this maneuver, we should still acknowledge and respect its original purpose.

DATA SUMMATION OF THE
TRAINING HORSE STANCE

Foot Position: Feet should be slightly wider than the width of your shoulders--toes in, heels out, Toe-Toe / Heel-Heel.

Weight Distribution: 50-50 - weight is forced out to outside edges of feet.

Reason and Purpose: To teach stamina and patience; a training stance which allows one to concentrate on hand movements only without being distracted by the synchronization of foot maneuvers.

Explanation: With feet shoulder width apart, clench both fists with palms up. Keep your head and back erect with your knees bent and forced out. It is from this stance that all other stances evolve.

DATA SUMMATION OF THE
FIGHTING HORSE STANCE

Foot Position: Both feet are pidgeon-toed with one foot ahead of, as well as directly behind the other. It is like a *Training* Horse with the opponent to the flank. Head and eyes are focused to the flank.

Weight Distribution: 50-50. Knees are forced away from each other.

Reason and Purpose: Minimize target areas, allow for a faster shuffle side or back kick.

Explanation: Get in a *Training* Horse Stance so that your body is at a 90 degree angle from your opponent. Keep your hands and arms in a fighting position.

BOW AND ARROW STANCE

BOW AND ARROW STANCE - There are four types of **BOW AND ARROW STANCES**; however, only three are important enough to describe in this text. They are the *NEUTRAL* **BOW AND ARROW STANCE** (or *NEUTRAL* **BOW**), *FORWARD* **BOW AND ARROW STANCE** (or *FORWARD* **BOW**), and *REVERSE* **BOW AND ARROW STANCE** (or *REVERSE* **BOW.**). They all serve useful purposes and should, therefore, definitely be added to your reservoir of knowledge.

WHY THE NAME BOW AND ARROW

I-32 The Bow and Arrow Stance was given this name because of the positioning of the stance. As you will notice, in the illustration shown above, when a Chinese Bow and Arrow Stance is superimposed on a Forward Bow Stance, they are almost identical. The forward or bent leg forms part of the bow and the rear or stiff leg represents the arrow.

NEUTRAL **BOW AND ARROW STANCE** - This **STANCE** has the advantage of the rear leg and arm easily being brought into play. It is a strong **STANCE** and since it is almost sideways, presents a small target. Consequently, the *NEUTRAL* **BOW** is a good **STANCE** for sparring. A major portion of class drill is placed upon perfecting the *NEUTRAL* **BOW** and it is also an important **STANCE** in executing techniques and forms (katas).

The *NEUTRAL* **BOW** is best compared with the *FIGHTING* **HORSE.** However, in this case, the feet are placed on either side of the line of sight, pointing to your opponent. Now without changing the position of your feet, pivot them in place so that they are pointing toward the front (see captions under photos below). Also rotate the waist a corresponding amount in the same direction. The result—a *NEUTRAL BOW AND ARROW STANCE* (see photos on pages **62** and **63**).

LP-1 Facing an opponent in the Fighting Horse Stance gives you a distinct defensive advantage, but limits your ability to retaliate effectively.

LP-2 The Neutral Bow is not as protective a stance, but in terms of effectiveness, it is much more versatile when employing defensive and offensive tactics.

Make note of the fact that the *NEUTRAL* **BOW** places the rear hip closer to the front than the *FIGHTING* **HORSE.** This is a crucial point of difference. It allows faster use of the rear arm and leg. The feet are pointed more toward the front and are parallel with one another instead of pigeon toed (see captions under photo on page **63**). The knees are still forced out and the weight rests equally on both feet.

ANALYTICAL STUDY
OF THE *NEUTRAL* BOW

FRONT VIEW

Position your arms so that the right arm covers the upper region and the left arm the middle region.

Have your head and eyes face the line of sight.

Since the body is almost sideways it presents a small target.

Your feet should be properly placed on either side of the line of sight -- left heel to the left of the line and the right toe to the right of the line.

Knees are forced out

Line of sight

TOP VIEW

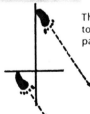

The feet are pointed more toward the front and are parallel to each other.

62

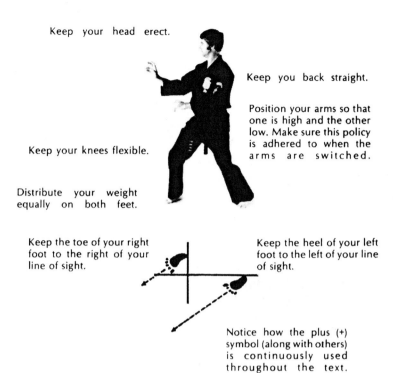

Keep your head erect.

Keep you back straight.

Position your arms so that one is high and the other low. Make sure this policy is adhered to when the arms are switched.

Keep your knees flexible.

Distribute your weight equally on both feet.

Keep the toe of your right foot to the right of your line of sight.

Keep the heel of your left foot to the left of your line of sight.

Notice how the plus (+) symbol (along with others) is continuously used throughout the text.

FINDING THE PROPER DIMENSIONS

To find the proper *width* of your *NEUTRAL* **BOW** (refer to illustrations on page **64**) have the heel of your rear foot line up with the toe of your forward foot. *Depth* can be found by dropping the knee of your rear leg so that it is in line with the heel of your forward foot (see illustration on page **64**). Once your *width* and *depth* are determined, have both knees bend naturally and the proper *height* will be arrived at automatically. Refer to the following illustrations for further elaboration.

A heel-toe relationship will aid you in finding your width.

You should be on the ball of your rear foot when you plant your knee.

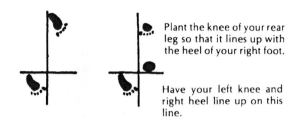

Plant the knee of your rear leg so that it lines up with the heel of your right foot.

Have your left knee and right heel line up on this line.

Have your right toe and left heel line up on this line.

A knee-heel relationship will aid you in finding your depth.

DATA SUMMATION
OF THE *NEUTRAL* BOW

Foot Position: One foot ahead of the other utilizing the Toe-Heel relationship to determine the proper depth. Both feet should run parallel to each other and at an angle of 45 degrees from your opponent.

Weight Distribution: 50-50.

Reason and Purpose: Gives you greater mobility, allowing you to retreat or advance with ease.

Explanation: With one foot ahead of the other, keep your back erect and your upper body at a 45 degree angle from your opponent. Your head should face forward on a 90 degree angle from your opponent. Position your arms so that your forward arm is high and your rear arm is low. See illustrations for further clarification.

FORWARD BOW AND ARROW STANCE - is primarily used in a **STANCE** change to extend the reach of the rear arm and increase its power. The most important contribution of the *FORWARD* **BOW** is as a **STANCE** change between *NEUTRAL* **BOWS.** The form and smoothness of this sequence will largely determine the effectiveness of the rear arm. Since retreating with the *FORWARD* **BOW** is difficult and exposure to vulnerable areas is more pronounced, this **STANCE** is intended to be transitory.

P-18a-d The photos appearing above show the various methods in which a Forward Bow Stance can be employed.

A *FORWARD* **BOW** (see photos on page 66) can be formed from the *NEUTRAL* **BOW** (see photos on page 62) by rotating the rear hip so that it is even with the forward hip. The front leg does not change, but the rear leg becomes almost stiff as it pushes the rear hip forward. The rear foot, while still flat, pivots on the ball (as the heel is thrust back) to a position where the toes point mostly forward (refer to page 66).

The weight shifts more to the front leg, but the tendency to lean with the shoulders or stiffen the forward leg, must be avoided. To check your form, watch yourself in a mirror. The movement is a rotation of the waist, the back remains straight, the shoulders square and parallel to the mirror, and the head does not rise nor move forward.

ANALYTICAL STUDY
OF THE *FORWARD* BOW

FRONT VIEW

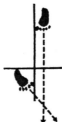

Your head does not raise up nor does it move forward.

Anchor your right elbow.

Have both of your arms in position to guard your vital areas.

The position of your front leg does not change. It is identical to your *Right Neutral Bow Stance.*

Keep your left leg parallel to the line of sight.

Line of sight

Keep your left foot parallel to your line of sight.

The position of your right foot is in the same position as when you are in a *Right Neutral Bow Stance.*

TOP VIEW

Have the heel of your left foot anchored to the ground.

Make sure your hips and shoulders are parallel to each other.

Focus your eyes straight ahead.

Make sure your shoulders are square and parallel to the mirror or wall in front of you.

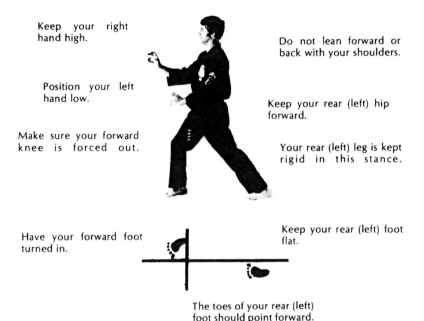

Keep your right hand high.

Do not lean forward or back with your shoulders.

Position your left hand low.

Keep your rear (left) hip forward.

Make sure your forward knee is forced out.

Your rear (left) leg is kept rigid in this stance.

Have your forward foot turned in.

Keep your rear (left) foot flat.

The toes of your rear (left) foot should point forward.

FINDING THE PROPER DIMENSIONS

Finding the proper dimensions for the *FORWARD* **BOW** are simple. First find the dimensions of your *NEUTRAL* **BOW** (see page 63). Once this has been determined, have the heel of your rear foot thrust back by pivoting on the ball of that foot. Push your rear hip forward, as you stiffen your rear leg so that both hips line up with each other. Upon completing this adjustment, all dimensions -- *width, depth* and *height* would be established automatically. See the following illustrations for further clarification.

67

FRONT VIEW

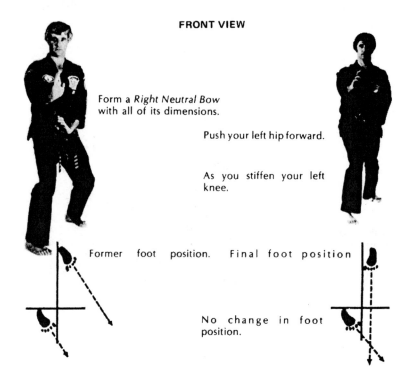

Form a *Right Neutral Bow* with all of its dimensions.

Push your left hip forward.

As you stiffen your left knee.

Former foot position.   Final foot position

No change in foot position.

SIDE VIEW

Have your hips line up with each other so that they are parallel to the front.

Have the heel of your rear (left) foot thrust back by pivoting on the ball of that foot.

Former foot position

No change in foot position.

DATA SUMMATION
OF THE *FORWARD* BOW

Foot Position: One foot is ahead of the other with your forward foot at a 45 degree angle from your opponent and the rear foot at a 90 degree angle from your opponent. Basically, a Toe-Heel/Heel-Knee relationship.

Weight Distribution: 60-40, 60% of your weight is on the forward leg and 40% is on the rear.

Reason and Purpose: Gives you greater reach, enhances your power, and allows you a greater foundation with which to brace yourself. It is useful as a leg check, buckle, or break.

Explanation: The FORWARD BOW originates best from a NEUTRAL BOW where the rear foot is positioned at a 90 degree angle from your opponent with the knee stiff. The weight is then increased on the forward leg as the upper body turns 90 degrees to your opponent along with your head and eyes. Your back and head are erect at this point.

REVERSE BOW AND ARROW STANCE — This STANCE is essentially the same as a *FORWARD* BOW with the head and shoulders turned to the back. As a STANCE change, the *REVERSE* BOW serves three primary purposes. First, it creates distance by pivoting away. Second, rotation can increase the power of certain movements and third, as the leg stiffens, it can buckle or sweep. There is a STANCE known as the *REAR* BOW, but it is used so seldom it does not merit discussion.

P-21a&b The photos shown above show how the Reverse Bow Stance can be utilized while striking.

69

ANALYTICAL STUDY
OF THE *REVERSE* BOW

FRONT VIEW

Have your rear arm protect your upper region.

Have your forward arm protect your middle region.

Keep your rear knee bent.

Keep your forward leg stiff.

Line of sight

TOP VIEW

Make sure your shoulders are parallel to your line of sight.

Keep your forward foot flat.

The foot position is the same as a *Forward Bow* with the exception that the head and eyes are turned into the oposite direction.

Have your head and eyes turn toward the opposite direction after establishing a *Forward Bow*.

Keep your rear arm high.

Keep your forward arm low.

Thrust your heel out and then anchor it to the ground.

Keep both feet flat.

FINDING THE PROPER DIMENSIONS

Again position yourself in the exact dimensions for a *NEUTRAL* **BOW**. However, form the *NEUTRAL* **BOW** in the opposite direction of your intended line of sight (see page 72). Immediately execute a *FORWARD* **BOW** while facing the same direction. Upon completion of the *FORWARD* **BOW**, have your head turn in the opposite direction (your intended line of sight). This final movement will automatically place you in a *REVERSE* **BOW** with all dimensions (*width*, *depth*, and *height*) adjusted to your own specifications.

Form a *Left Neutral Bow* with all of its related dimensions while facing in the opposite direction of your intended line of sight.

Now form a *Left Forward Bow* while facing in the same direction.

Turn your head to your right and focus your eyes toward the intended or final line of sight.

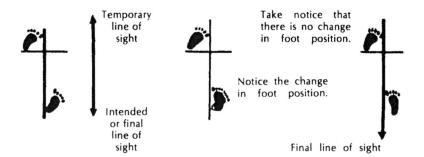

Temporary line of sight

Intended or final line of sight

Take notice that there is no change in foot position.

Notice the change in foot position.

Final line of sight

DATA SUMMATION
OF THE *REVERSE* BOW

Foot Position: One foot is ahead of the other with the forward foot at a 90 degree angle (heel out) from your opponent and the rear foot at 45 degrees (heal out). This stance is the opposite (reverse) of a *FORWARD* BOW with your head and eyes turned toward your opponent.

Weight Distribution: 40-60 -- 40% of your weight is on the forward leg and 60% on the rear leg.

Reason and Purpose: Allows one greater distance although remaining in place. Gives greater power using opposing force; is useful as a leg check, buckle, or break.

Explanation: The *REVERSE* **BOW** stems best from a *NEUTRAL* **BOW** where the forward leg is stiff and locked from the hip to the ankle as the rear leg is kept bent. The *REVERSE* **BOW** is essentially the same as a *FORWARD* **BOW** with the head and shoulders turned back.

KNEEL STANCE

KNEEL STANCES — are of two types -- *WIDE* and *CLOSE*. The major difference between the *WIDE* and *CLOSE* **KNEELS** is the space between the knees. The feet are basically the same distance apart in *width* (as a *NEUTRAL* **BOW**), but may vary in *depth*, depending upon the circumstances.

Three facts explain its use. First, the body drops in *height* thereby giving power to a downward strike (principle of *Gravitational Marriage*), avoids an attack, or reaches a low target. Second, as with most **STANCE** changes, there is usually a rotation of the hips and shoulders which can boost the force of the horizontal blow. The combination of change in *height* plus the rotation will increase the effectiveness of a strike moving diagonally downward. Third, the rear knee drops down and may, therefore, act as a weapon, as a check (pin), or as a push to buckle an opponent's leg.

Although the *Wide* **KNEEL** has greater stability, the fact remains that a *CLOSE* **KNEEL** can be extremely useful offensively as well as defensively. Both should not be overlooked since they are definitely "alphabets of motion" that can help increase your "vocabulary of motion".

WIDE **KNEEL STANCE** — This **STANCE** is no more than a *NEUTRAL* **BOW** with the rear knee dropped and forced out. There is no change in the positioning of the front leg or foot. However, the rear heel is raised off the ground to allow the knee to bend down further. Both knees are forced apart -- hence the name, *WIDE* **KNEEL**. The **STANCE** is quite low, the weight equally divided between the two feet, and the back is straight.

ANALYTICAL STUDY
OF THE *WIDE* KNEEL

FRONT VIEW

Keep your right arm low.

Keep your eyes straight ahead.

Make sure your knees are forced apart.

Keep your left arm high.

Have your weight equally distributed on both legs.

Keep your forward foot positioned in the same position as that of your *Neutral Bow.*

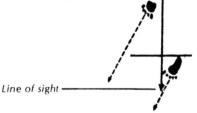

Line of sight ————

TOP VIEW

30°

Keep your shoulders in line with your hips.

Your rear leg is at a 30° angle to your line of sight.

Keep your body parallel to the wall or mirror in front of you.

Keep your head erect.

Keep your back straight.

Place your hands and arms in guard position.

Keep your buttocks tucked in.

Make sure the heel of your rear (right) foot is off the ground.

Keep your forward foot flat.

Keep the ball of your right foot on the ground.

FINDING THE PROPER DIMENSIONS

First find the proper dimensions for a *NEUTRAL* **BOW**. Now bend, drop, and force your rear knee out on a 30 degree angle from your upper body which is vertical and erect. Make sure your rear knee is one hand span (your hand) from the ground. Although the *width* and *depth* of this **STANCE** is the same as a *NEUTRAL* **BOW** (even though the rear heel is raised), a hand span measurement should aid you in obtaining the proper *height* for the **STANCE**.

Form a *Left Neutral Bow* with all of its dimensions.

Bend and drop your right knee while forcing it out and away from you on a 30° angle.

The depth is the same as a *Neutral Bow*.

Your rear (right) knee should be one hand span from the ground. This measuring method will aid you in finding your proper height.

Raise your heel.

The ball of the foot remains the same width as a *Neutral Bow.*

DATA SUMMATION
OF THE *WIDE* KNEEL

Foot Position: Forward foot is at a 45 degree angle to opponent, rear foot at a 45 degree angle from your opponent resting on the ground. Like a *NEUTRAL* **BOW**, only your body drops in position.

Weight Distribution: 50-50 -- rear knee is forced out.

Reason and Purpose: The drop in height gives added power (*Gravitational Marriage*), avoids an attack, better access to low targets, can act as a pin or check, and gives greater stability.

Explanation: From a *NEUTRAL* **BOW**, drop your height and weight by bending the knee of your rear leg so that your weight rests on the ball of your rear foot with the knee and weight of your rear leg forced out. There is basically no change required of the front leg or foot. The stance is quite low, the weight equally divided and the back is straight.

CLOSE **KNEEL STANCE** — This **STANCE** is no more than a *Forward* **BOW** with the rear knee dropped one to two inches from the ground. The *width* remains the same, but the *depth* may fluctuate by sliding the rear foot foward on your line of sight. This, of course, would depend on the circumstances. Like the *WIDE* **KNEEL**, there is no change in the positioning of the front leg or foot and the rear heel is also raised off the ground to allow that knee to bend freely. The forward knee is the only one forced out. The rear knee is kept in and close to the forward leg -- hence the name, *CLOSE* **KNEEL**. The **STANCE** is exceedingly low, the weight equally divided between the two feet, and the back is kept straight. The *CLOSE* **KNEEL** is lower than the *WIDE* **KNEEL** since the rear knee is kept closer to the ground. The weight, though equally distributed, is centered over the rear knee.

ANALYTICAL STUDY
OF THE *CLOSE* KNEEL

FRONT VIEW

Keep your eyes straight ahead.

Keep your left arm high.

Keep your right arm low.

Force your forward (left) knee out.

Have your rear (right) knee brought straight down.

Have your weight distributed equally on both legs.

Your forward foot should be positioned identically to that of a *Left Neutral Bow.*

TOP VIEW

Your shoulders should be in line with your hips.

Make sure your rear (right) leg is parallel to your line of sight.

Line your body so that it is parallel to the wall or mirror in front of you.

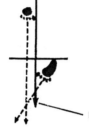

Line of sight

SIDE VIEW

Keep your back straight.

Keep your head erect.

Make sure your arms and hands are in guard position.

Tuck your buttocks in.

Raise your right heel off of the ground.

Keep your forward (left) foot flat.

Keep the ball of your right foot on to the ground.

Keep your right knee one to two inches off of the ground.

Line of sight

79

FINDING THE PROPER DIMENSIONS

The first step is to find the proper dimensions for a *FORWARD BOW*. Once obtained, bend and drop your rear knee straight down toward the floor and about one to two inches from it. Make sure your rear knee does not touch the ground. Although the *width* and *depth* of this **STANCE** is the same as a *FORWARD* **BOW** (even though the rear heel is raised), having your rear knee one to two inches from the ground should aid you in obtaining the proper *height* for this **STANCE**.

SIDE VIEW   **FRONT VIEW**

Form a *Right Forward Bow* with all of its proper dimensions.

Bend and drop your left knee straight down so that it parallels the vertical angle of your head.

Your rear (left) knee should be two inches from the ground.

The distance between the feet remain the same as the *Forward Bow.*

Raise your left heel.

DATA SUMMATION
OF THE *CLOSE* KNEEL

Foot Position: Forward foot is at a 45 degree angle to opponent; rear foot is at a 90 degree angle to your opponent resting on the ball of the foot with the heel off the ground. Rear foot may shuffle forward if an adjustment is needed. Like the FORWARD **BOW**, only your body drops in position.

Weight Distribution: 50-50. Rear knee is dropped straight down so that it parallels the vertical angle of your head.

Reason and Purpose: The drop in height gives added power (*Gravitational Marriage*), avoids an attack, allows for better access to low targets, can act as a pin, check, or be used to fracture, gives instant stability.

Explanation: From a FORWARD **BOW**, drop your height and weight by bending the knee of the rear leg so that your weight rests on the ball of your rear foot. There is basically no change required of the front leg or foot. The stance is quite low, the weight equally divided, the back and head straight, and the rear knee one to two inches from the ground.

TWIST STANCE

TWIST STANCES — are of two types -- *FRONT* and *REAR*. Both have numerous applications. They are more commonly used as a means to advance or retreat without rotating the trunk of the body. Or, they may be used as **STANCE** changes to protect the groin, to break a leg, to check, or to switch the forward and rear arms without shifting the feet. They can be assumed on the follow through for a sweep or kick. And, on occasion, they may be used as deceptive moves when freestyling.

TWISTING is a short term for **TWISTED HORSE** so called because the **STANCE** is readily formed from a **HORSE** by twisting the waist and allowing the feet to pivot freely.

A good **TWIST** sits quite low and maintains half the weight on the ball of the rear foot. With practice, both **TWIST STANCES** can be held comfortably since strength comes from resting one knee on the calf of the other.

FRONT **TWIST** — An easy method to position into a *FRONT* **TWIST STANCE** (other than twisting into it from a **HORSE**) is to start from a **LEFT** *NEUTRAL* **BOW** and have the rear (right) foot slide directly forward and past the front foot while the toes of the rear (right) foot continue to point off to the side. As your weight moves forward, the heel of the stationary (left) leg comes off the ground permitting the knee of the same leg to bend forward until it rests on the calf of the right leg. The right foot lies flat on the floor. The feet are now basically at right angles -- a little less than the width of a **HORSE STANCE** apart. Positioned in this *FRONT* **TWIST**, the shoulders or hips do not rotate and the maneuver prior to establishing the *FRONT* **TWIST** is called a *RIGHT FRONT CROSSOVER*.

ANALYTICAL STUDY
OF THE *FRONT* TWIST

FRONT VIEW

Keep your eyes and head focused forward.

Keep your right arm low.

Keep your right foot flat.

Distribute your weight equally on both legs and feet.

Keep your left arm high.

Have your left knee rest on your right calf. Do not allow any space between your legs (thighs).

Have your left foot rest on the ball of the foot only.

TOP VIEW

Keep your hips in line with your shoulders.

Your right foot should also be parallel to wall of mirror in front of you.

Keep your upper torso on a 45° angle to the wall or mirror in front of you.

Line of sight

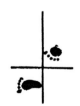

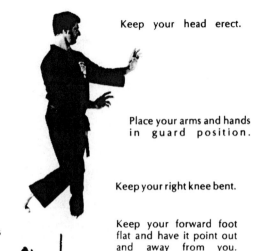

Keep your head erect.

Keep your back straight.

Keep your buttocks tucked in.

Place your arms and hands in guard position.

Bend your left knee and have it rest on the center of your right calf.

Keep your right knee bent.

Make sure your left heel is off the ground.

Keep your forward foot flat and have it point out and away from you.

FINDING THE PROPER DIMENSIONS

First find the proper dimensions for a **LEFT** *NEUTRAL* **BOW**. Now slide the rear (right) foot directly forward and past the front (left) foot so that it is approximately half the distance or *width* of what a **HORSE STANCE** would be for you. This maneuver will aid you in obtaining the proper *width* and *depth* of your *FRONT* **TWIST STANCE**. To obtain the proper *height*, rest your left knee on the calf of your right knee and drop your body weight so that it securely rests on your right calf.

This maneuver will aid you in obtaining your proper *width* and *depth*.

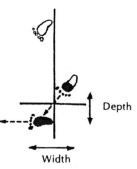

Depth

Width

(1) From a *Left Neutral Bow*.

(2) Slide your right foot directly forward and past your left foot so that it is approximately half the distance or width of a *Horse Stance*.

This maneuver will aid you in finding your proper *height*.

Do not allow any space between your legs.

(3) Drop your body weight so that your left knee securely rests on top of your right calf.

85

DATA SUMMATION
OF THE *FRONT* TWIST

Foot Position: Forward foot is parallel to opponent and placed flat on the floor. Rear foot is on a 45 degree angle to your opponent and on the ball of that foot.

Weight Distribution: 50-50. 50% of the weight is on the forward leg --50% on the rear leg.

Reason and Purpose: Used in transition when going either forward or backward. Allows for a fast drop in height, used to stomp with, to conceal the rear leg prior to kicking with it; protects the groin, assists in breaking a leg, as a check, or used as a sweep.

Explanation: An easy method to obtain the *FRONT* **TWIST** is to start from a *NEUTRAL* **BOW STANCE** and have the rear foot slide directly forward and past the front foot while the toes of the rear foot (which was originally the forward foot) continues to point off to the side. As your weight moves forward, the heel of the rear leg comes off the ground permitting the knee to bend forward until it rests on the calf of the forward leg. The forward foot lies flat. When the **TWIST STANCE** is produced in this manner, the shoulders or hips do not rotate and the maneuver is called a *FRONT CROSS-OVER*.

A good *FRONT* **TWIST STANCE** sits quite low and maintains an equal weight distribution.

REAR **TWIST** — A *REAR* **TWIST STANCE** can also be positioned from a **LEFT** *NEUTRAL* **BOW** by having the rear (right) foot slide directly to the back of and past (ahead of) the front (left) foot while the toes of the rear (right) foot continue pointing in the same direction. As the weight moves forward, the stationary (left) foot remains flat as the rear (right) foot is planted on the ball of that foot. Have the right knee rest on the calf of the left leg. When the *REAR* **TWIST** is produced in this manner, the shoulders or hips, like the *FRONT* **TWIST** do not rotate and the maneuver prior to establishing the *REAR* **TWIST** is called a *RIGHT REAR CROSS-OVER*.

ANALYTICAL STUDY
OF THE *REAR* TWIST

FRONT VIEW

Keep your eyes and head focused forward.

Guard with your left arm high and your right arm low.

Place your right knee on your left calf. Do not allow any space between your knees and thighs.

Keep your left foot flat.

Plant the ball of the foot only.

Balance your weight equally on both of your legs.

TOP VIEW

Have your hips line up with your shoulders.

Place your body on a 45° angle to the wall or mirror in front of you.

Place your left foot on a 45° angle to the wall or mirror in front of you.

Have your right foot face you in a vertical and upright position.

Line of sight

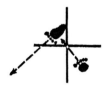

Keep your head erect.

Keep your back straight.

Tuck your buttocks in and sit low.

Place your arms and hands in guard position.

Bend your left knee.

Bend your right knee.

Raise your right heel off ground.

Have your right foot point in and toward you.

Have your left foot point away from you.

FINDING THE PROPER DIMENSIONS

Like the *FRONT* **TWIST**, find the proper dimensions for a **LEFT** *NEUTRAL* **BOW**. This time, slide the rear (right) foot directly to the back of and past (ahead of) the front (left) foot so that it again travels approximately half the distance or *width* of a **HORSE STANCE** for you. This maneuver will aid you in obtaining the proper *width* and *depth* of your *REAR* **TWIST STANCE**. From this position, drop your body weight so that your right knee rests securely on top of your left calf -- thus, your proper *height* is obtained.

This Maneuver will aid you in obtaining your proper *width* and *depth*.

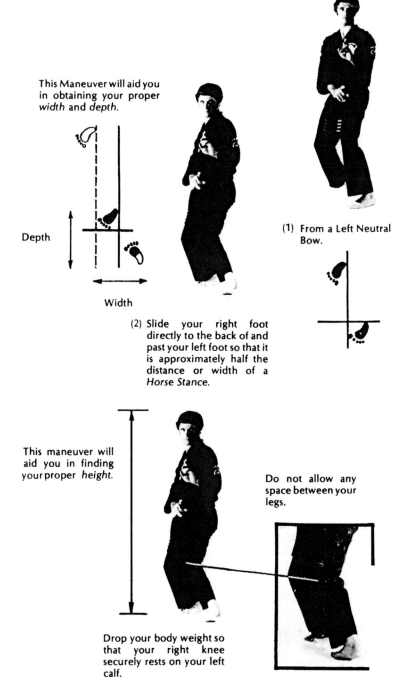

Depth

Width

(1) From a Left Neutral Bow.

(2) Slide your right foot directly to the back of and past your left foot so that it is approximately half the distance or width of a *Horse Stance*.

This maneuver will aid you in finding your proper *height*.

Do not allow any space between your legs.

Drop your body weight so that your right knee securely rests on your left calf.

DATA SUMMATION
OF THE *REAR* TWIST

Foot Position: Forward foot (lead foot) is at a 45 degree angle from opponent resting on the ball of that foot. Your rear foot (originally the forward foot) is parallel to your opponent and resting flat.

Weight Distribution: 50-50. 50% of the weight is on the forward leg and 50% on the rear leg.

Reason and Purpose: Used in transition when going either forward or backward, allowing for a fast drop in height, used to stomp with, to break or check, and to protect the groin.

Explanation: An easy method to obtaining the *REAR* **TWIST STANCE** is to start from a *NEUTRAL* **BOW STANCE** and have the rear foot slide directly back of and past (ahead of) the forward foot so that the weight rests on the ball of that foot (which was originally the rear foot) and points on a 45 degree angle to your opponent. As the weight is equally distributed on both legs, allow the knee of the present lead leg to bend and rest on the calf of the present rear leg. The rear foot (formerly the forward foot) lies flat. When the **TWIST** is produced in this manner, the shoulders or hips do not rotate and the maneuver is called a *REAR CROSS-OVER*.

CAT STANCE

CAT STANCE also consists of two types -- *45°* and *90°* **STANCES.** In both of the **CAT STANCES,** the forward leg rests lightly and is poised for a kick. Shifting the weight off the front leg also provides a defense against a possible leg sweep. (A sweep is an attempt to knock a victim's supporting leg out from under him using your leg or foot to do so.) With approximately 90% of the body weight centered low and on the rear leg, it is this very strain on the rear leg that explains, in part, why these two types of **CAT STANCES** are usually transitory.

45° **CAT** — While executing this **STANCE**, the rear foot is flat and points off to the side at a 45° angle with the knee bent facing the same direction. Since the thighs in this **STANCE** are relatively close together, the 45° **CAT** in *FOOT MANEUVERS* is used to protect the groin. The ball of the front foot (while resting on the ground) is in line with the rear heel (see page 90) and placed far enough forward so that a side view (see page 90) shows the shin a little less than vertical.

ANALYTICAL STUDY OF THE 45° CAT

FRONT VIEW

Your eyes and head should face straight ahead.

Keep your right arm low.

Keep your left arm high.

Keep your thighs relatively close together.

Remain flat on your right foot.

Plant the ball of your left foot only.

Keep 90% of your weight on your right foot.

10% of your weight should be on your left foot.

Keep your body parallel to
the wall or mirror in front
of you.

Your hips should be
in line with your
shoulders.

Your left foot
should be on a 90°
angle.

Your right knee and
foot should be on a
45° angle.

Line of sight

SIDE VIEW

Keep your back straight.

Keep your head erect.

Have your buttocks
tucked in and make sure
that it sits low.

Have your arms and hands
in guard position.

Bend your left knee.

Bend your right knee.

Make sure your left heel is
raised off the ground.

Make sure that both of
youreet are pointed away
from you.

Your left foot is on a
90° angle.

Your right foot is on
a 45° angle.

OTHER HELPFUL INFORMATION

There are many variations of the **CAT STANCE**. The primary difference generally involves the forward foot although the constant factor is that very little weight is placed upon it. You may position the foot so that it rests on (a) the ball of the foot, (b) flat of the foot, or (c) the heel of the foot. Regardless of what is used, they basically serve the same purpose.

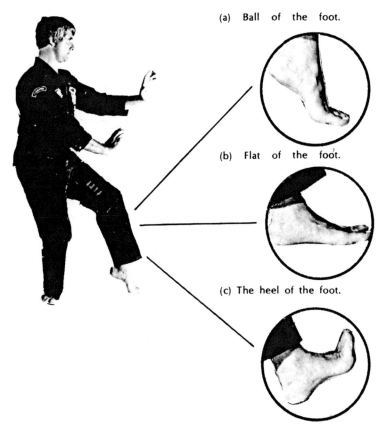

(a) Ball of the foot.

(b) Flat of the foot.

(c) The heel of the foot.

SPECIAL NOTE: According to history, practitioners often placed their bare feet on the ground in any one of the three variations thus illustrated to feel the ground vibrations of approaching men or horses.

FINDING THE PROPER DIMENSIONS

A helpful aid in finding the proper dimensions for a 45° **CAT** is to use the plus (+) symbol to visually assist you. Place strips of masking tape on the floor to form a plus (+) with equal lengths. Position the rear foot so that the foot points out on a 45° angle (see illus. below). Place the heel of your forward foot against the heel of your rear foot (see illus. below). Now proceed to lift your forward foot and scratch a parallel and imaginary line where the big toe of that foot ends (see illus. below). Lift your forward foot and place the heel of that foot on the imaginary line that was just mentally drawn. Place 10% of your weight on the ball of your forward foot and lean back so that the remaining 90% of your weight rests on your rear leg.

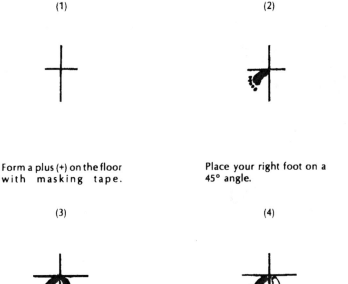

(1)

Form a plus (+) on the floor with masking tape.

(2)

Place your right foot on a 45° angle.

(3)

Place your left heel in line with and along side of your right heel -- this will give you the proper *width* for this stance.

(4)

Draw an imaginary line where your left big toe ends.

Lift your left foot and plant the foot forward so that the heel of your left foot is where your big toe formerly ended--this will give you the proper *depth* for this stance.

Place 10% of your weight on the ball of your left foot and 90% of your weight on the right foot. Bend your knees comfortably and you will then obtain the proper *height* for this stance.

DATA SUMMATION OF THE 45° CAT

Foot Position: The toes and foot of your forward leg are on a 90° angle to your opponent with the rear foot at a 45° angle to your opponent. They are 45° from each other.

Weight Distribution: 10-90. 10% of the weight is on the forward leg --90% on the rear leg.

Reason and Purpose: Useful in transition. Poised for a kick, better used against a frontal attack, useful defensively as well as offensively. Forward leg cannot be easily upset by a sweep.

Explanation: The body sits fairly low on the rear leg. The rear foot is flat and points off to the side at a 45° angle with the knee bent in the same direction. The forward foot rests lightly (ball of foot only) with toes and foot pointed straight ahead (90° to opponent). The ball of the foot is in line with the rear heel.

90° CAT — The rear foot is flat in this **STANCE**; however, the difference is the direction of the toes and foot which point off to the side at a 90° angle with the knee bent in the same direction. The thighs in this case are not close together as the *45° **CAT**. This **STANCE** normally occurs from a surprised flank attack where there isn't enough time for the rear foot to shift into a 45° angle. With time being the primary factor, the forward foot is the only leg that is activated. When this occurs, the rear foot remains at a 90° angle to the forward foot. There is no protection to the groin because of the legs being so wide and apart; therefore, other hand positions are necessary to compensate for this. The ball of the front foot is also in line with the rear heel (see illus. below) and placed far enough forward so that a side view (see next page) shows the shin a little less than vertical.

ANALYTICAL STUDY OF THE *90°* CAT

FRONT VIEW

Keep your eyes and head focused straight ahead.

Keep your right arm low.

Keep your left arm high.

Make sure that your thighs are apart rather than together.

Keep your right foot flat on the ground.

Plant the ball of your left foot.

Place 90% of your weight on your right foot.

Place 10% of your weight on your left foot.

TOP VIEW

Your body should be parallel to the wall or mirror in front of you.

Line your hips with your shoulders.

Make sure your right knee and foot are on a 90° angle.

Line of sight

SIDE VIEW

Keep your head erect.

Keep your back straight.

Place your arms and hands in guard position.

Keep your buttocks tucked in and make sure it sits low.

Keep your left knee bent.

Raise your left heel off the ground.

Make sure that both feet are pointed away from you.

Your left foot is also on a 90° angle.

Your right foot is on a 90° angle.

FINDING THE PROPER DIMENSIONS

Again place masking tape on the floor to form a plus(+). This time have your rear foot point out on a 90° angle (see illus. below). As with the 45° **CAT STANCE**, the heel of your forward foot is placed against the heel of your rear foot (see illus. below). Lift your forward foot and draw and imaginary line with the big toe of that same foot. Lift your forward foot and place the heel of that foot on the imaginary line that was mentally drawn. Place 10% of your weight on the ball of your forward foot and lean back and over your rear leg so that the remaining 90% of your weight rests on that leg.

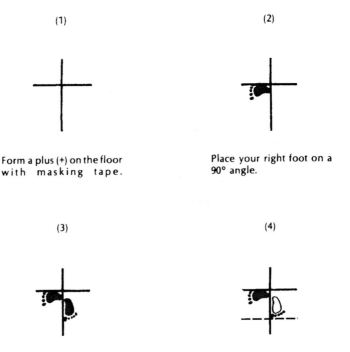

(1)

Form a plus (+) on the floor with masking tape.

(2)

Place your right foot on a 90° angle.

(3)

Place your left heel in line with and along side of your right heel -- this will give you the proper *width* for this stance.

(4)

Draw an imaginary line where your left big toe ends.

Lift your left foot and plant
the foot forward so that
the heel of your left foot is
where your big toe was
formally -- this will give
you the proper *depth* for
this stance.

Place 10% of your weight
on the ball of your left foot
and 90% of your weight on
the right foot. Bend your
knees comfortably and
you will then have the
proper *height* for this
stance.

DATA SUMMATION OF THE *90°* CAT

Foot Position: The toes and foot of your forward leg is at a 90° angle
from your opponent with the rear foot parallel to your opponent (90°
to your forward foot and leg). Both are 90° from each other.

Weight Distribution: 10-90. 10% of the weight is on the forward leg
--90% on the rear leg.

Reason and Purpose: This stance is useful in transition when you are
poised for a kick. It is best used against a flank attack. It is useful
defensively as well as offensively. It would be difficult to upset your
forward leg with a sweep.

Explanation: The body sits fairly low on the rear leg. The rear foot is
flat and points off to the side at a 90° angle with the knee of the same
leg bent in the same direction. The forward foot rests lightly (on the
ball of the foot) with toes and foot pointed straight ahead (90° to
opponent). The ball of the front foot is in line with the rear heel.

ONE LEG STANCE

ONE LEG STANCES are of various types. The name is self-explanatory. What constitutes a *right* or *left* ONE LEG STANCE does differ from the other STANCES mentioned in this Chapter. In each case, it is the supporting leg (leg bearing the body weight) that determines a *right* or *left* ONE LEG STANCE. The air-borne leg (leg which is raised) is not used as a determining factor because of the numerous positions, directions, and heights it can be placed in.

P-35 A montage of various poses and postures utilizing the One Leg Stance.

ONE LEG STANCES are commonly used while jumping from side to side to avoid a frontal or rear atack. It may stem from a CAT STANCE you are positioned in to ward off a leg sweep. Generally, it is a very useful transitional STANCE while shifting from one STANCE to another. On occasion, it may be used deceptively while freestyling. The hand positions can also vary depending upon the ONE LEG STANCE position used.

IMPORTANT NOTE: A ONE LEG STANCE can be formed by raising the rear leg instead of the forward leg. It does not have to be the forward leg.

ANALYTICAL STUDY OF THE ONE LEG

FRONT VIEW

Have your eyes and head focus straight ahead.

Keep your left arm high.

Keep your right arm low.

Lift your left leg up and in the air.

100% of your weight is on your right foot.

Keep your right foot flat.

TOP VIEW

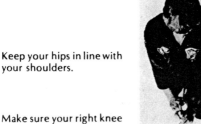

Keep your body parallel to the wall or mirror in front of you.

Keep your hips in line with your shoulders.

Position your left knee on a 90° angle.

Make sure your right knee and foot are on a 45° angle.

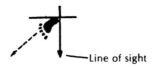

Line of sight

Keep your head erect.

Keep your back straight.

Make sure your arms and hands are in guard position.

Keep your bottocks tucked in and have it sit low.

Bend you left knee and 'raise it to waist level.

Bend your right knee.

Make sure both feet are pointed away from you.

Even with your left foot in the air it should still face on a 90° angle.

Position your right foot on a 45° angle.

FINDING THE PROPER DIMENSIONS

Two of the dimensions *width* and *depth*, are missing. *Height* is really your only concern in executing a **ONE LEG STANCE**. In executing a **ONE LEG STANCE**, bend your supporting leg to a comfortable and balanced position and maintain it. Make sure that your entire weight is centered on your supporting leg. You can execute a **ONE LEG STANCE** from any of the **STANCES** mentioned in this Chapter. Cock your leg (suspended leg) to any height or position. Turn your head in any direction and place your hands and arms in any position -- you would still be positioned in a **ONE LEG STANCE**.

From a *Left Neutral Bow* or
any desired stance.

Lift your left (forward) leg
in the air.

With your left (forward)
leg in the air, center your
entire weight on your right
leg (supporting leg) and
bend your right knee to a
comfortable and balanced
position.

DATA SUMMATION OF THE ONE LEG

Foot Position: Your leg is suspended and your knee points to the left
or right. The rear leg is bent with the foot at a 45° angle (from a **LEFT
NEUTRAL BOW**) to your opponent. The rear leg can be raised
instead of the forward leg if desired.

Weight Distributions: 100% on supporting leg.

Reason and Purpose: Used more to protect the groin area. Utilizes
economy of motion when executing a side kick with the leg that is
suspended in the air.

Explanation: Forward (or rear) leg is cocked in the air with the heel next to the knee of the supporting leg (this is not a hard or fast rule). The supporting leg should be bent with your body weight directly above the supporting leg to maintain maximum balance. Your back should be erect and arms in a guarding position.

IMPORTANT NOTE

In forming the aforementioned **STANCES**, further clarification is needed to determine what constitutes a *left* or *right* **NEUTRAL BOW** (*FORWARD* and *REVERSE*), **KNEEL** (*CLOSE* and *WIDE*), **TWIST** (*FRONT* and *REAR*), **CAT** (45° and 90°), etc. With the exception of the **ONE LEG STANCES**, a *left* or *right* **STANCE** is so named to designate the lead leg in addition to the direction you are facing (both head and eyes) at the time each **STANCE** is established. The only exception rests with the **ONE LEG STANCE**. The reason is obvious. The leg that is suspended in the air can be found in a number of directions and *does not* under any circumstance support the body weight. Therefore, it is the leg supporting the body that should be credited and determines whether the **STANCE** is *left* or *right.*

CHAPTER 7
MANEUVERS

MANEUVERS are unique strategic methods used to evade and/or attack an opponent. It involves traveling techniques using an array of foot work patterns in addition to changing body positions and posture. Employing these methods can aid you in creating or decreasing distance (to your best advantage), can be used preceding an attack, used simultaneously with an attack, or used after an attack. This is done by *stepping, shuffling, crossing, twisting, hopping, jumping,* and *leaping* with your legs, or by *feinting, turning, riding, rolling, slipping, bobbing* and *weaving* using the upper torso and other necessary combinations. The directions and combinations of your **MANEUVERS** are many; nevertheless, circumstances can place limitations upon them.

Movements incorporating the legs are classified as *FOOT* **MANEUVERS** or methods employed to move about in any direction utilizing **STANCES**. These methods are further broken down into subdivisions and types.

Step Throughs are steps used while advancing, retreating or moving to the left or right sides. Thus, we have the *Forward Step Through,* the *Reverse Step Through,* and the *Side Step Through* (left and right).

Shuffles are combinations of *drags* and *steps,* or vice versa. They consist of four basic types -- *Drag Step, Step Drag, Push Drag,* and *Pull Drag. Like the Step Throughs,* the traveling direction of a *shuffle* can be *Forward, Reverse,* or to the *Side.*

Crossovers[1] are combinations of over exaggerated *drags* and normal *steps.*

---

1. There is a great similarity between a **FRONT** and **REAR CROSSOVER** and a **FRONT** and **REAR TWIST STANCE**. The key difference is *continued motion.* A **FRONT** and **REAR CROSSOVER** incorporates an additional step. No sooner do you go into a **FRONT** or **REAR CROSSOVER** then you step out with an additional step to complete the **MANEUVER** (motion). A **FRONT** or **REAR TWIST STANCE** remains motionless for a period of time. It is exactly the same as a **FRONT** and **REAR CROSSOVER** minus the additional step that completes the **MANEUVER** (motion).

Crossovers fall into two categories -- Front Crossovers, where one leg crosses over and in front of the other, and *Rear Crossovers,* where one leg crosses behind and back of the other. *Front* and *Rear Crossovers* can be done while *advancing* or *retreating. Hopping, Leaping, Jumping,* and *Diving* are other **MANEUVERS** that can be used. These methods will be elaborated upon when the techniques themselves are described.

After you have thoroughly learned these *FOOT* **MANEUVERS,** they can aid you in developing rapid angle changes, increasing or decreasing distance, adding greater power to your strikes or blows, and helping to nullify your opponent's actions. Their importance cannot be over emphasized and must be incorporated to assure maximum efficiency.

In taking a closer look at *FOOT* **MANEUVERS,** we find them to be intricate adding sophistication to the Art. *Sophisticated Moves* are single moves that produce dual or multiple results. In contrast, *Embryonic Moves* only achieve a single effect. They may consist of single moves or multiple moves, but only a single effect is achieved.

Consider the following example. If a *Step Through* **MANEUVER** brought your foot along side of your opponent's leg and then you proceed to *Buckle* his leg (see following illustrations), this action would have required two movements to accomplish a single effect and thus be considered *Embryonic.* In contrast, if your *Step Through* **MANEUVER,** following the correct angle, went directly through the opponent's leg to *Buckle* him in a single move (see same illustration), it would have given you the desired distance as well as caused your opponent's leg to *Buckle.* In short, it would have been a single move with a dual effect and, therefore, *Sophisticated.*

P-36a&b (a) Place your right leg alongside of as well as inside of your opponent's right leg; and (b) have your right knee reach over to buckle your opponent's right knee out and away from him.

P-37 Rather than stepping alongside of your opponent's right knee and then buckling it, make it a one step action by simply stepping through your opponent's leg to cause it to buckle.

A more detailed study of *FOOT* **MANEUVERS** proves even more interesting. Other then the *Buckle*, *FOOT* **MANEUVERS**, coupled with **STANCE CHANGES**, can be used to *Check, Pin, Lock, Spread, Sprain*, or *Break* various parts of an opponent's anatomy. Combinations of these methods can also be employed if desired, depending upon the circumstances or the dictates of one's conscience. For example, you can use a *Step Through Reverse Foot* **MANEUVER**, pivot into a *Right Wide* **KNEEL STANCE** to *Buckle* your opponent's leg, make an *in place* **STANCE CHANGE** while dropping into a left *CLOSE* **KNEEL STANCE** to *break* your opponent's ankle (see following photos for clarification). When *FOOT* **MANEUVER** combinations are properly synchronized with combinations using the limbs of the upper torso, proficiency is enhanced and victory increasingly assured.

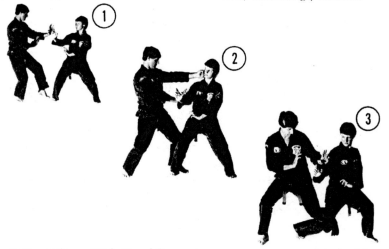

P-38 Utilize a Wide Kneel Stance to cause your opponent to buckle.

P-39 Switch (inplace) into a Close Kneel Stance with exuberance and utilize your Close Kneel Stance to break your opponent's ankle by vigorously dropping your knee on his ankle.

Movements incorporating the *upper* torso of the body are classified as *BODY* **MANEUVERS**. It can also be defined as methods employed to move in any direction using the *upper* torso. Like *FOOT* **MANEUVERS**, *BODY* **MANEUVERS** can be subdivided into types of moves. However, it must be emphasized that many of the *BODY* **MANEUVERS** are coordinated with *FOOT* **MANEUVERS** or vice versa and; therefore, to completely isolate one from the other would be unrealistic. Further, although the *upper* torso may be utilized more often then the legs, the legs; nevertheless, can incorporate these same methods on a limited scale, or use them in a slightly altered pattern.

Turning is one of the methods used to maneuver the body to *avoid, ride,* or *slip* pass a punch, kick, or strike. In addition to using it as a defense, it can also be used to increase the effectiveness of an offense. Using sophistication *Turning* can be defensive and offensive simultaneously. To *avoid* an attack, *BODY* as well as *FOOT* **MANEUVERS** may be employed. In more technical terms, *Turning* is a slow version of a *Twist;* nevertheless, both methods aid in torquing.

Riding a punch, kick or strike primarily refers to having your head or body go with an attack. In the process of doing so, distance is maintained, or at least attempted, however slight it may be. To accomplish this method, *retreating* is often used. When one *retreats* simultaneously while *Turning,* it is labeled *Rolling. Rolling* is a combination of both *Riding* and *Turning.*

Slipping is a sophisticated method of *avoiding* a punch, kick or strike. It does not need to involve *Turning* or *Rolling* to be effective, although it may employ these **MANEUVERS** if the situation warrants it. *Slipping* is simply a method of *avoiding* a punch, kick, or strike with or without the use of a defensive block. In other words, a block is not necessary when your proficiency is at its peak. The head or body *avoids* the attack by fractions of an inch as it *slips* and *advances toward* your opponent to counter attack, crowd, jam, check, or frustrate him.

Bobbing is a verticle or *diagonal* method of motion used to *avoid, duck,* or *slip* past a punch, kick, or strike. It is the *up* and *down* or *down* and *up* motion used to *avoid* or initiate an attack. It can be accomplished by bending at the waist or knees or by using a combination of both. *Ducking* is the downward motion of *Bobbing.* It is practically a straight drop. *Weaving* involves a *horizontal* or *diagonal* method of motion which is used to *avoid* or *slip* pass a punch, kick or strike. It is the *left* to *right, right* to *left* or *side* to *side* motion used to *avoid* or initiate an attack. The waist and knees can be used independently or in combination with each other as the feet remain basically in place. A combination of *Bobbing* and *Weaving,* increases your versatility, maneuverability and effectiveness when you are being evasive or when you are counter attacking. One proficient in *Bobbing* and *Weaving* can be extremely elusive.

Feinting is the use of deceptive gestures or maneuvers to lure or cause your opponent to react. It is a *set-up* move employed as part of your intended plan of action. It is used to mislead and deceive your opponent so that your counter or follow-up action can then be effectively executed, delayed, or eliminated entirely. Specific parts of the body such as the head, shoulders, arms, or even the legs are used for *Feinting.* A *feint* can be a simple gesture, a pronounced action, or it can be a number of gestures used consecutively in a variety of time periods to create the desired results. *Feints* against the unskilled are not as necessary as against the skilled; however, they can cause a dramatic reaction to your plan of attack.

The information contained in this and future volumes covers a vast array of experiences. It is for the novice as well as the advanced practitioners; therefore, you are cautioned to practice only those exercises paralleling your ability.

Ed Parker

ORGANIZATIONAL CHART ON MANEUVERS

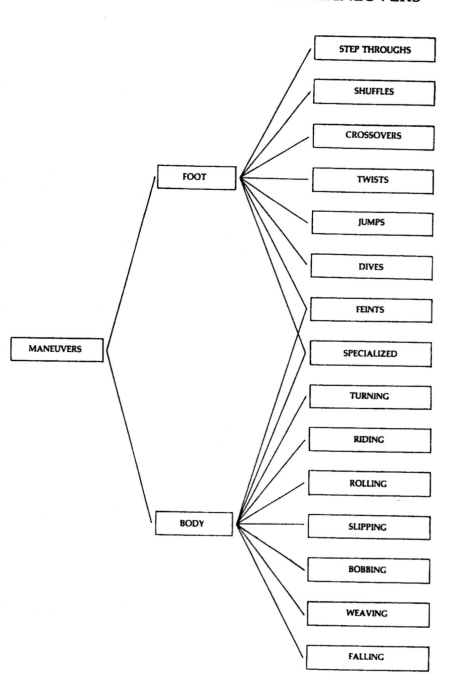

ORGANIZATIONAL CHART
ON FOOT MANEUVERS

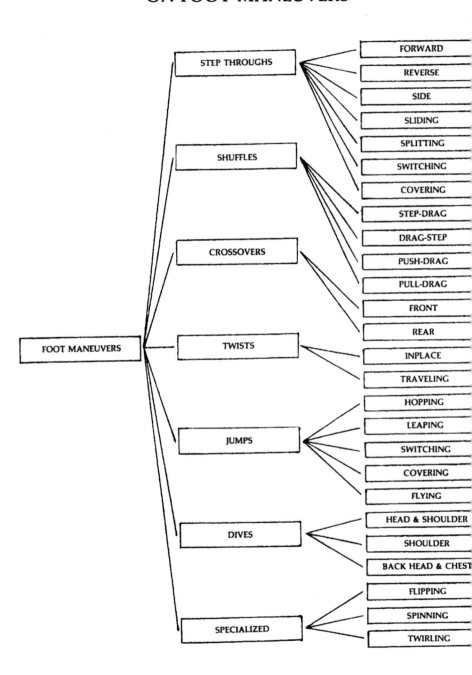

FOOT MANEUVERS

STEP THROUGHS are *steps* used to **MANEUVER** *forward, back* (in *reverse*), to the *side* and other directional angles while evading or attacking an opponent. They are generally *walking steps* (steps that leave the ground before being replanted). However, they can also employ such methods as *sliding, splitting, switching* and *covering* in completing the *step*. These *steps* can be full, half or quarter steps, depending upon the desired effect. The following illustrations and descriptions should help clarify each of the methods used for *STEP THROUGHS.*

From an Attention Stance (1) step forward with your left foot into a Left Neutral Bow Stance (2) and then step forward with your right foot (3) into a Right Neutral Bow.

From an Attention Stance (1) step back with your left foot into a right Neutral Bow Stance (2) and then step back with your right foot (3) into a left Neutral Bow Stance.

ANOTHER INTERESTING COMPARISON

As you execute your **FOOT MANEUVERS**, think of your head as a gyro on a ship's compass. A gyro, if you are acquainted with one, remains uneffected by the pitching and rolling movement of a ship. No matter how rough the water or what position the ship may be forced into, the gyro remains parallel with the horizon. Therefore, while executing your **FOOT MANEUVERS**, change your body positions, but not your head. Allow your head and eyes to focus in the direction that you're moving to or from. Although this policy is generally practiced, there are, nevertheless, always exceptions to the rule.

Allow your head to act as a gyro on a ship's compass.

SLIDING is a method of executing a *step* using one foot at a time. In this maneuver, the foot is kept in constant contact with the ground. Like other methods, SLIDING steps can move *forward, back* or to the *side* while starting or finishing the desired maneuver. While SLIDING, the head is kept level so that Bobbing is minimized. Every *action* becomes direct thus, economically executed. Balance and *stability* are also enhanced along with *power* and *impact*.

When *sliding,* your steps can move forward, back, or to the side. Your foot, however, should be kept in constant contact with the ground.

SPLITTING can be best described as *two SLIDES* simultaneously executed. In other words, both feet simultaneously *slide* apart from each other. Its primary purpose is to cause an instant drop in height to avoid an attack, execute an attack, or while using combinations of both. Under rare conditions, it may be effective in actual combat. However, it is not recommended for the novice practitioner. It is valuable as an exercise in *stretching* the legs and not so much as an aggressive or defensive technique.

When applying *splits*, limberness is an important factor.

SWITCHING entails a combination of *steps*, or a *jump* to change **STANCE POSITIONS** while remaining in the same spot and facing in the same direction. There are two methods of *SWITCHING* -- one employs *STEP THROUGHS* and the other a *JUMP. SWITCHING* is often used to better position oneself, to protect vital target areas, to enhance an attack, to be deceptive, and to enhance one's strategy.

SWITCHING utilizing *STEP THROUGHS* are of two varieties --REAR-TO-FRONT and *FRONT-TO-REAR. REAR-TO-FRONT* requires that your lead or forward foot moves back (in line with your rear foot) then your rear foot immediately steps forward so that it is in the position your forward foot was. *FRONT-TO-REAR* requires that your rear foot moves forward (in line with your lead or forward foot). Immediately step back with your forward foot so that it is where your rear foot was. See illustrations. The *JUMPING SWITCH* (third variation) will be described under the heading of *JUMPS.*

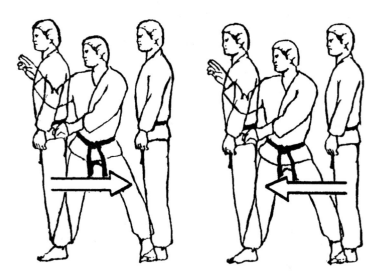

When *switching,* you can move your left foot back then your right foot forward.

OR

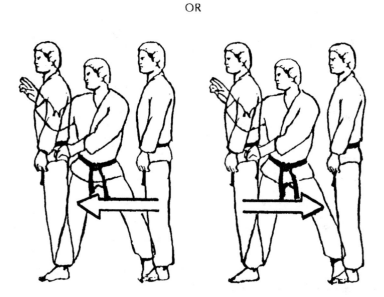

You can have your right foot move forward and then your left foot back.

COVERING is a *STEP THROUGH* method used to turn and face in the opposite direction. The lead foot *steps* to the opposite side then turns in the opposite direction. It is strongly recommended when one is planning to turn in the opposite direction because of the built-in safety factor that it offers. In the process of completing this motion, your body actually *retreats* from the initial attack. In other words, you actually move *away from* rather than *toward* it. Unable to see what is back of you nor the type of attack being used, it would be foolish to move *toward* his action. Such a move would only speed up your opponent's action and add to his force. See illustrations.

Move your right foot (1) to your left (2) while still facing the same direction.

Now turn counterclockwise (3) and face the opposite direction.

SHUFFLES are related methods of *dragging* or *scraping* the feet combined with *steps*, *pushes*, or *pulls* to *shift* from one location to another. There are *four SHUFFLE* combinations using the feet and leg muscles to *shift* the body (*forward*, *back*, or to the *side*) with either foot in the lead. The left foot could be ahead of the right foot or the reverse when employing any one of the *SHUFFLES*.

A *STEP-DRAG SHUFFLE* can be best executed by:

(3) Now drag your left foot forward so that the same distance is maintained between your feet as step (1).

(2) Step forward with your right foot into a deeper *Right Neutral Bow.*

(1) Get into a *Right Neutral Bow and . . .*

(4) From your *Right Neutral Bow . . .*

(5) Step back with your left foot into a deeper *Right Neutral Bow.*

(6) Now drag your right foot back so that the same distance is maintained between feet as step (4).

119

As you will note from the previous illustrations, you can execute a FORWARD STEP-DRAG SHUFFLE or a REVERSE STEP-DRAG SHUFFLE with your *right foot* as the *lead foot* (the foot that is forward prior to the execution of your move). The same moves can apply should your *left foot* be the *lead foot*.

A DRAG-STEP SHUFFLE is the *reverse* order of a STEP-DRAG SHUFFLE and can be done easily by:

(3) Complete the move by having your right foot step forward so that the same depth is maintained as step (1).

(2) Have your left foot drag forward so that the depth of your stance is decreased.

(1) Form a *Right Neutral Bow*, then . . .

The description given was that of a *forward* DRAG-STEP SHUFFLE. The following best describes how to execute a *reverse* DRAG-STEP SHUFFLE.

(1) Form a *Right Neutral Bow Stance*, then . . .

(2) Have your right foot drag back so that the depth of your stance is decreased.

(3) Complete the move by having your left foot step back so that the same depth is maintained as step (1).

Both *forward* and *reverse* DRAG-STEP SHUFFLES can be done with the *left* foot in the lead.

In my estimation, the most important *SHUFFLE* is the *PUSH-DRAG SHUFFLE*. It can be executed faster than any of the other *SHUFFLES* triggering instant momentum and thus creating immediate *back-up force*. The result -- greater contact impact. Although speed can be kept constant while you are moving *forward* or *back*, the *PUSH-DRAG SHUFFLE* is at maximum effectiveness moving *forward*. However, under special circumstances, where your opponent is well within the range of your *natural weapons* maximum force can be obtained while *retreating* with the *PUSH-DRAG SHUFFLE*.

The following best describes how to execute a *PUSH-DRAG SHUFFLE*.

The Push Drag Shuffle requires that you lift your forward leg slightly off the ground and push forward with the rear or supporting leg. The supporting leg in turn drags after you so that the original distance before commencing the Push Drag Shuffle reoccurs again. The Push Drag in reverse requires that you raise the rear leg and push back with the forward leg. The forward leg then drags after you so that the distance between the feet is the same as before commencing the maneuver.

The *PULL-DRAG SHUFFLE* is primarily used by the more adept to slip a kick in on an opponent as the supporting leg (the leg bearing your weight) is literally *pulled* into action in order to allow your body to lunge forward. This particular *SHUFFLE* is often confused with the *STEP-DRAG SHUFFLE* and requires practice to perfect. With practice and experience, the difference between a *PULL-DRAG* and *STEP-DRAG SHUFFLE* will become obvious. As a final statement, it can be said that a *STEP-DRAG SHUFFLE* is embryonic while the *PULL-DRAG SHUFFLE* is sophisticated.

The following best describes how to execute a *PULL-DRAG SHUFFLE*.

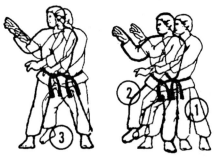

(1) From a *Right Neutral Bow Stance* . . .

(2) Slightly left your right foot so that it is barely off the ground.

CROSSOVERS are combinations of over-exaggerated *drags* and normal *steps* -- an instantaneous **FOOT MANEUVER** in conveying an attack to an opponent or retreating from him. *CROSSOVERS* allow you to create and adjust distances. Because of the length of distance that this maneuver can cover, it is considered a *long range* **FOOT MANEUVER**. Used as an offensive maneuver, it allows for faster and deeper penetration. As a defense, it assures you a safe distance from your opponent.

CROSSOVERS fall into two categories -- *FRONT CROSSOVERS*, where one leg crosses over and in front of the other; and *REAR CROSSOVERS*, where one leg crosses behind and in back of the other. Both methods can be done while *advancing* or *retreating*.

A *FRONT CROSSOVER* can be best executed by:

When proceeding forward have your left foot step in front of, as well as forward of your left leg. Flatly plant your left foot while raising the heel of your right foot. Your body weight should be evenly distributed at this point. Then step forward with your right foot into a right Neutral Bow Stance.

(3) Immediately have your body weight lunge forward as your left foot is pulled and dragged with the shifting of your body weight.

(4) As your body lunges forward you can then (a) plant your right foot into a *Right Neutral Bow Stance,* or (b) take advantage of the momentum of your body weight and execute a right kick.

When proceeding in reverse with the Front Crossover have your right foot step back, but in front of your left foot. Flatly plant your right foot while raising the heel of your left foot. Your body weight is again evenly distributed at this point. Continue your foot maneuver by stepping back with your left foot and position yourself into a right Neutral Bow Stance.

A *REAR CROSSOVER* can be best executed by:

HISTORICAL INTEREST

While *CROSSOVER MANEUVERS* work well on flat terrain, history records that it was originally developed to effectively travel up and down stairs. (See illustration.) With practice, you will also discover the ease with which you can travel up and down stairways using *CROSSOVERS*. This **FOOT MANEUVER** is indeed practical. Thus, my philosophy -- if tradition can be applied today, use it, if not, *store it; but do not discard it.*

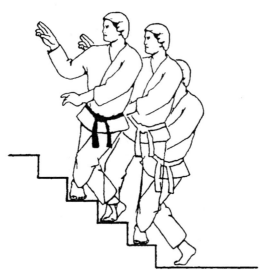

Crossovers can enhance travel up or down stairways.

Rear *Crossovers*, forward or reverse, are executed like the front *Crossovers* except the leg crosses behind of, rather than in front of the supporting leg.

TWISTS are methods of *turning* the body with the aid of the feet and legs, to evade an attack, or contribute to the force of your offense. There are two types -- *INPLACE* and *TRAVELING TWISTS*. The following illustrations and descriptions should suffice in clarifying both.

The *INPLACE TWIST* requires simultaneous body and leg *rotation*. In the execution of this *TWIST*, the body not only *turns*, but *drops in height* as well. In analyzing the *INPLACE TWIST*, you will notice that the maneuver from a *NEUTRAL BOW STANCE*, triggers an *inward action* that is, your body turns toward you while remaining in place. The advantages of using this maneuver either *defensively* or *offensively* are great even as you *drop into* this *TWIST*. Yet, advantages of both *defense* or *offense* can also be gained while *unwinding* from the *INPLACE TWIST*. The torque from such an action can render surprising results.

Now let us proceed to illustrate and describe the *INPLACE TWIST*.

From a (1) left Neutral Bow, execute an inplace counterclockwise pivot and settle into a left Front Twist Stance.

125

(1) Form a *Left Neutral Bow Stance*.

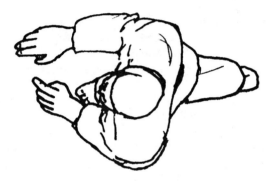

(2) Begin to turn counter-clockwise with your left and right foot plus your upper body.

(3) Complete your rotation by fully turning counter-clockwise so that your left foot is parallel to the front, 50% of your weight is on the ball of the right foot and your right shoulder is pushed forward and in front your left shoulder.

NOTE: Reverse your motion and you will unwind the *Inplace Twist* and go back into a *Left Neutral Bow Stance*. Violent action created by this move can be converted into a profitable offense.

TRAVELING TWISTS are not very common, but should be added to your storehouse of knowledge. Depending upon how your feet are positioned, you can move from side to side or forward or back diagonally employing your lead foot. Its primary use is to *stalk* an opponent and secondly to *avoid* an attack.

The *TRAVELING TWIST* consists of two varieties -- *NATURAL* and *EXAGGERATED*. *Close examination of the NATURAL* version may cause controversy for it tends to resemble a *turn* more than a *twist*. Nevertheless, the difference is so slight that I have categorized it as a *TWIST*. The *EXAGGERATED* version leaves no doubt that it is in fact a *TWIST*. When applied, the lower half of the body shows obvious contortion compared with the upper body. This obvious contortion is characteristic of a basic *TWIST*.

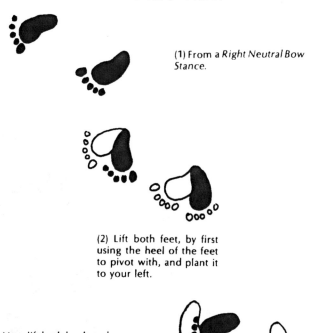

(1) From a *Right Neutral Bow Stance.*

(2) Lift both feet, by first using the heel of the feet to pivot with, and plant it to your left.

(3) Now lift both heels and pivot to your left on the ball of each foot and then plant them.

NOTE: Step (2) could have started off by pivoting on the ball of each foot first then the heels.

Upper body faces the same direction as the lower half of the body.

Lower half is basically in synch with the upper half, thus there is not a noticeable difference in the direction that both halves face.

Normal Version

Upper body does not face the same direction as lower half.

Lower half faces left as upper half faces right.

Exaggerated Version

JUMPS are methods of having your feet or foot leave the ground *getting to* or *away from* an opponent. Although the feet or foot leaves the ground in executing a *JUMP*, they, nevertheless, remain *at* or *below* the level of your *waist* or *head*. There are several types of *JUMPS* -- *HOPS, LEAPS*, a *SWITCHING JUMP* (a *jump* that is made while facing in the same direction), and *FLYING JUMPS*. There are many variations of *HOPS, LEAPS* and *FLYING JUMPS*. Only the essential *JUMPS* will be discussed, described and illustrated in this Chapter.

HOPS are one leg *JUMPS* that require a minimum of height to execute. They somewhat resemble a *PULL-DRAG SHUFFLE* with the exception that the foot does not *drag* on the ground. It becomes slightly airborne before the foot is planted and the body repositioned.

The primary purpose of a *HOP* is to rapidly close the distance between you and your opponent. As the *HOP* is executed, every effort is made to protect the vital areas of the body.

(2) Pick up your left foot and balance your weight on your right leg.

(3) Jump forward with your right foot on to the same foot.

(1) From a *Right Neutral Bow Stance* . . .

(4) Plant your left foot forward into a *Left Neutral Bow Stance.*

LEAPS are *explosive JUMPS* used to evade or attack an opponent. They require vigorous effort in acquiring a fair degree of height. While executing this move, both feet may simultaneously leave the ground, or you may use one foot at a time. No matter what method is employed, both feet do become airborne during the course of a *LEAP*. Having the feet leave the ground at different time periods does not alter the fact that both become airborne at a particular point in time.

ONE-LEG LEAPS require one foot leaving the ground at a time with both becoming airborne prior to the planting of your feet or foot. Whatever foot is planted, the weight of the body balances and rests on that leg. This *LEAP* is primarily used as an evasive maneuver that positions your body for the next counter.

(1) From a Left Neutral Bow Stance . . .

(2) Leap forward and to your left on a 45° angle. Use your right foot to push off with.

(3) Land on your left leg keeping your left knee flexible and balance your weight on your left leg as you form a *Left One-Leg Stance.*

TWO-LEG LEAP -- involves both feet simultaneously leaving as well as being planted on the ground. It is mainly used as an offensive maneuver to give added height to the final move employing *gravitational marriage.*

(1) From a standing position

(2) Leap forward using both legs to push off with.

(3) Land on both legs keeping your knees flexible so as to enhance your balance.

SWITCHING JUMP -- This is the third method used to *SWITCH STANCES*. See page. 118   paragraph   2   . However, instead of using *STEP THROUGHS* to accomplish the *SWITCH*, a *JUMP* is executed to achieve the same results. This method requires *jumping* in the air, *switching* your legs, reversing their order in mid-air, landing on the identical spot and facing in the same direction. Like the other two *SWITCHING* methods, it can be used to better position yourself, minimize your target areas, enhance your attack, act as a deceptive maneuver, and be of benefit strategically.

(1) From a Left Neutral Bow. . .   (2) Jump up in the air . . .   (3) And switch legs and body (slightly) while in the air.   (4) Land on the identcal spot, facing the same direction and into a *Right Neutral Bow Stance.*

COVERING JUMP -- is a *JUMPING* method, instead of a *STEP THROUGH* method, used to turn and face in the opposite direction. Here again, not seeing what is behind you nor the type of attack being used, this method affords you the opportunity of turning in mid-air and facing in the opposite direction while actually retreating from an unknown action.

(2) Jump up into the air and begin to turn counter-clockwise.   (3) Complete the 360° turn in mid-air. . .

(1) *From a Right Neutral Bow.* . .

(4) And land with both feet into a *Left Neutral Bow Stance* while facing the opposite direction.

FLYING JUMPS are JUMPS that are not only airborne, but that travel or sail through the air as well. They can be activated from *dead standstill* or from a *running start*. They too may be used to avoid an attack or aid your attack. Used strictly as a *defense*, it is called FLYING JUMP. Converted into an *offense*, it changes from a FLYING JUMP (which it starts off as) to a FLYING KICK (there are different types -- FLYING BACK KNUCKLE STRIKE, etc.). Used as an *offense* the body becomes almost parallel to the ground at the point of execution.

(1) From a standing position jump with both legs. Stretch them out as you sail through the air. Recock your legs and plant them into a standing position.

(2) From a running position jump in the air with both legs, cock them in mid-air and turn counterclockwise as you deliver a *Right Knife-edge Kick*, recock your legs and land on both feet.

FURTHER ADVICE

Please use caution in executing these exercises. Caution can never be overemphasized if you are not a gymnast.

Get assistance with the following exercises from someone who is knowledgeable or experienced in gymnastic capabilities.

Ed Parker

DIVES are unique methods that use exaggerated moves to avoid an attack, work in conjunction with an attack, or as a defense-offense combination. Because they are unique, DIVES are categorized separately. Employing elements of a JUMPS, DIVES are, nevertheless, unquestionably different. The key difference exists between height levels of the head and feet. In a DIVE, the head lunges forward followed by the feet. At a certain period during a DIVE, the feet are raised above the level of the head. It is this relationship of height -- the feet being higher than the head -- that separates a DIVE from a JUMP. Technically speaking, it could be said that a DIVE is a complete JUMP. However, for purposes of clarity, the two will be kept

The *HEAD AND SHOULDER DIVE* involves a straight forward motion, *DIVING* head first, tucking the head, then rolling equally on the shoulders, back, hips, buttocks, and feet.

Notice the level of the feet is higher than the head.

From a standing position (a) bend your knees and dive head first with hands outstretched to break your fall. As you can see, the feet are raised above the level of the head (b) with your hands helping to break your fall,

SHOULDER DIVE involves turning the body on a slight angle so that either the right or left side of the body is used to roll with. If you decide to use the right, you will partially roll with the right arm, shoulder, hip, thigh, and get back on your feet.

Again notice the level of the feet is higher than the head.

From a standing position (a) bend your knees and dive and turn to your right with your right arm outstretched to help break the fall. Again the feet are higher than the head (b) with your right arm helping to break separate.

Another distinguishable difference between a *DIVE* and *JUMP*, involves body parts that make contact with the ground at the time of execution. Executing a *JUMP*, you leave the ground with your feet and land on them. When *DIVING*, you leave the ground with your feet and land on your hands (in the majority of cases), then roll with the body using parts of your arm, shoulder, back, hip, and leg before landing up on your feet again.

There are three main types of *DIVES* -- *HEAD AND SHOULDER*, *SHOULDER*, and *BACK, HEAD, AND CHEST*. Other specialized *DIVING* methods and their uses will be described in future works.

tuck your head, roll on your shoulders, back, hips, and buttocks and have the momentum carry you forward and back on to your feet. You then have the option to *Cover* if you wish.

your fall, tuck your head toward your left shoulder and roll on your right shoulder, hip, thigh, and get back on to your feet.

BACK, HEAD AND CHEST DIVE -- This is a straight *DIVE* to the rear. It is not a common *DIVE* and, therefore, requires practice. To execute it, spring back on to your hands, keep your head and back arched, and time your action carefully as you roll on your chest, stomach, hips, thighs, knees, and feet.

Your feet are above the level of your head.

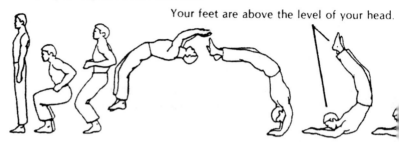

From a standing position (a) bend your knees, squat, and spring backward; reach out with your arms to break your fall. Arch your head and back, and again bend your knees. As your hands touch the ground,

---

FLIP -- is a *SPECIALIZED FOOT MANEUVER* employed to move the feet from one spot to another. Contained within a *FLIP* are elements of a *JUMP, DIVE,* and *HAND SPRING.* It is executed in three steps --from *feet* to *hands* and back to *feet.* The wrists play an important role in executing a *FLIP* since it acts as a springing device that aids you

---

The *FRONT FLIP* starts off like a *HEAD AND SHOULDER DIVE,* lands on the hands, and springs you back on to your feet.

From a standing position, squat down, leap forward with your arms outstretched, and land on your hands. The instant you make ground con-

straighten your body (b) as your weight begins to shift over the center point, again arch your head and back. Now begin to roll on your chest, stomach, hips, thighs, knees, and feet.

---

in completing your maneuver. Although it is an acrobatic maneuver, it is useful and can be strategically used as a primary method of escape. It can also aid you offensively or as a defense-offense combination.

Two types of *FLIPS* will be discussed -- *FRONT* and *BACK*.

tact with your hands, use your arms and wrists to flip you over and back on to your feet again.

The *BACK FLIP* starts off like a *BACK HEAD AND CHEST DIVE*, lands on the hands, and springs you back on to your feet again.

From a standing position, squat down, leap backward with your arms stretched out behind you, and land on your hands. The instant you make

---

SPINNING is a *specialized foot maneuver* used to escape from or attack an opponent. Its distinctive feature is that the feet are in constant contact with the ground. Both the legs and upper body are synchronized with each *spin* to enhance the momentum and speed of the attack or escape. It is, nevertheless, not a common maneuver for beginner students, but a must for those of higher training. Every

---

SPINS can be executed while rotating *clockwise* or *counterclockwise* -- going *toward* or *away from* your opponent. It goes without saying that circumstances and your personal skill dictates your choice of action.

From a standing position, bend your knees slightly (to aid your balance during the maneuver) and move either clockwise or counterclockwise by stepping off with either your right or left foot. If you step off with your right foot, (going counterclockwise and in a forward motion) plant your

Like the Front Flip, your feet are above the level of your head.

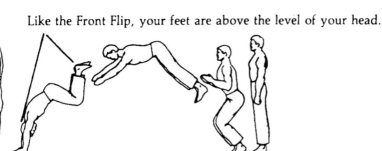

ground contact with your hands, use your arms and wrists to flip you over and on to your feet again.

---

alphabet of motion should be learned. The greater your vocabulary of motion, the less likely that you will miss opportunities as they arise. Remember, opportunities to attack or escape must never be overlooked. Learn every aspect of motion whether it is to be used offensively or defensively. A point to remember -- *every move when reversed can be an answer to an offense or defense.*

right foot to your left, while *SPINNING*, and continue to *SPIN* by moving your left foot in a backward motion and plant it to the right of your right foot. Further distance could be covered by continuing the same procedure.

TWIRLING -- Although this *specialized foot maneuver* is similar to *SPINNING* in appearance, it warrants a descriptive term of its own because it is executed while *airborne*. It is literally a *SPIN* to turn your body *clockwise* or *counterclockwise* while in the air; traveling from one ground point to another. Both the upper and lower body are

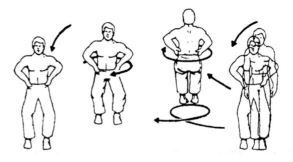

From a standing position, bend your knees slightly (to aid your balance during the maneuver) and jump either clockwise or counterclockwise

HURDLING, another *specialized foot maneuver*, describes jumping over obstacles to get from one ground point to another. In combat, it may require jumping over a stool, chair, person, etc. as part of your defensive or offensive strategy. The fact that these jumps are encumbered by obstacles makes the maneuver challenging and unique. *HURDLING* often employs several combination jumps --*leaping, flying* and occasionally *covering*. Only the highly skilled should use this in combat. Beginners should walk or run around the obstacles and use them as a means of defense.

Only the highly skilled should leap over obstacles such as a chair.

synchronized to *TWIRL* simultaneously while moving toward or away from your opponent. It could further be said that a *TWIRL* is no more than a *TURNING* **JUMP**. It, too, is primarily taught to advanced students.

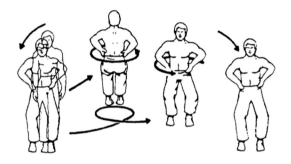

TURNING 360° in the air and landing on both feet You may continue this action more than once.

VAULTING -- This *specialized foot maneuver* requires a prop such as a staff, table, an opponent's body or other like objects to support, launch, and execute a jump from one ground point to another. The fact that props are needed for support in launching the jump makes it special and unique. During the launch, two choices are available (1) only planting the feet, or (2) kicking with the feet before planting them. The highly skilled are the only ones who should employ this method in combat.

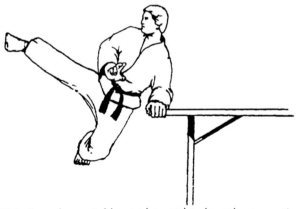

Objects such as a table can be used to launch your action.

ORGANIZATIONAL CHART
ON BODY MANEUVERS

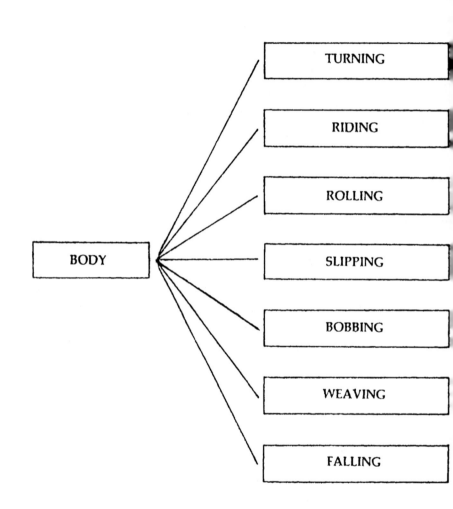

BODY MANEUVERS

TURNING is a method of rotating the upper body to the left or right while in place. The *turn* normally occurs within a 180° radius. It, too, can be used to avoid an attack, or counter attack while simultaneously avoiding an attack. *TURNING* can be done while on the ground.

RIDING is a method of having your upper body go with an attack. This could be done while standing in place or while retreating with the foot.

ROLLING is a method of avoiding an attack using a *ride* and *turn* combination. A *ROLL* extends beyond a 180° radius and up into a 360° radius. Having the same flexibility as other methods, you can *ROLL* with an attack while simultaneously counterattacking. *ROLLING* can be done in place or coordinated with **FOOT MANEUVERS**. *ROLLING* can also be executed on the ground.

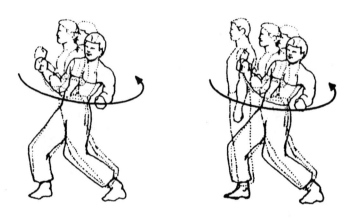

SLIPPING is a method of avoiding an attack while going toward your opponent's action. This may be done directly or indirectly. That is, you can *SLIP* pass and toward your opponent at the very start of an attack or *RIDE* the attack first, before *SLIPPING* toward the action. A counter can accompany a *SLIP*.

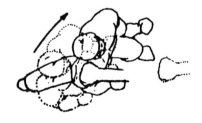

BOBBING is a method of avoiding an attack while vertically dropping underneath or rising above the action of your opponent. This maneuver aids you in positioning yourself below (also known as ducking)• or above the level of your opponent's attack. Again a counter could accompany a *BOB*.

WEAVING is a method of avoiding an attack while horizontally moving the upper body from side to side (toward a number of angles). Countering while *WEAVING* can also be accomplished.

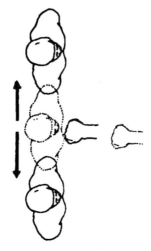

FALLING is an exaggerated method of *RIDING* an attack. The major difference is you constantly remain on your feet while *RIDING*, and you either rest on your back or stomach when *FALLING*. When on the ground from a *FALL, TURNING* or *ROLLING* can be applied and coordinated with a counter.

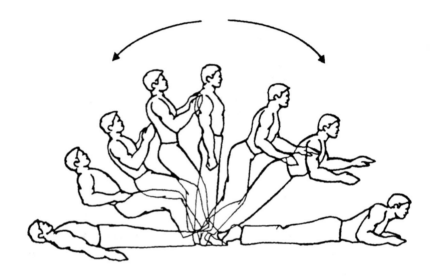

CHAPTER 8
CONCLUSION

I have been told that there are basically three types of people that make up this world:

1. Those who *make it happen;*
2. Those who *let it happen;* and
3. Those who *ask, what happened?*

You, therefore, must ask yourself which of these three categories apply to you. If it is number one, the material in this and subsequent volumes will be learned without question since *making it happen* would classify you as a *doer.* As one *does* he inevitably takes command of his subject. Taking command evolves to mastery of the subject. When this occurs the following proverb would then apply, "If you wish to know the road ahead, inquire of those who have traveled it." Underlings would seek counsel from you because it is you who have traveled the road ahead.

There are so many sayings that are apropo to our daily living. The following statement is a good example, "Those who can, *do.* Those who can't, *teach.* Those who neither can, nor can't, become *critics.*" Which of these statements apply to you? Are you one who *can,* or are you a teacher, or critic? It falls on your shoulders to make the choice.

DON'T QUIT

When things go wrong, as they sometimes will,
When the road you're trudging seems all uphill,
When the funds are low and the debts are high,
And you want to smile, but you have to sigh,
When care is pressing you down a bit;
Rest if you must, but don't you quit.

Life is queer with its twists and turns,
As every one of us sometimes learns,
And many a failure turns about
When he might have won had he stuck it out.
Don't give up though the pace seems slow;
You may succeed with another blow.

Often the goal is nearer than
It seems to a faint and faltering man;
Often the struggler has given up
When he might have captured the victor's cup;
And he learned too late when the night slipped down,
How close he was to the golden crown.

Success is failure turned inside out,
The silver tint of the clouds of doubt
And you never can tell how close you are,
It may be near when it seems afar;
So stick to the fight when you're hardest hit,
Its when things seem worst that you mustn't quit.

Unknown

GLOSSARY OF TERMINOLOGY

"AND -- a word in our Kenpo vocabulary that is eliminated by the more adept. It involves time and therefore is contradictory to economy of motion - a principle well worth following.

BLOCK -- a defensive maneuver used to hinder or check an attack.

BY-THE-NUMBERS -- methods used to teach beginners the basics. Each step is given a number. This is similar in principle to using phonics.

CHECK -- to restrain, hinder, or repress an opponent from taking action. This is accomplished by pressing, pinning, or hugging an opponent usually at the joints so that it minimizes his leverage and nullifies his actions.

CLOCK PRINCIPLE -- a system, in teaching, which was developed by Ed Parker to help the student to visually imagine the direction which he is to follow. He is generally asked to think of himself as being in the middle of a big clock facing 12 o'clock with 6 o'clock to the rear, 3 and 9 to his right and left and all other numbers in their respective places.

CONDITIONED RESPONSE -- to conform and respond instanteously to given variable.

DOUBLE FACTOR -- it entails a duel movement of defense which can incorporate any combination of blocks, parries, and checks. It also refers to sophisticated moves which are duelly defensive and offensive. It involves the utilization of reversing motion as an answer in defending or attacking--thus opposite as well as reverse motion, both supply answers in combat.

FEINT - a misleading move used to deceive an opponent.

JUMP -- a maneuvering method which involves moving forward, back, or sideways by vigorously springing or leaping to avoid or execute an attack.

LEAP -- a springing type jump for purposes of evasion or attack.

LINE OF SIGHT -- the path of a moving target brought into alignment.

MANEUVER -- a method which you use to close or extend your range.

MATHEMATICAL AND GEOMETRIC SYMBOL CONCEPTS -- This concept can be paralleled with the clock principle and, therefore, each method can be used interchangeably thus providing similar results and benefits.

MUMBLING MOTION -- movements that are not distinct in application. They can be compared with words that lack diction.

PHYSICAL PREPAREDNESS -- all phases of preventive planning to avoid a confrontation.

SOPHISTICATED SIMPLICITY -- basic movements that entail more than the eyes can see, though singular in appearance, they are multiple in action.

STEP-DRAG -- stepping forward or back with one foot as the other drags to meet it. This is one of the three methods of executing a shuffle.

STEP THROUGH -- the execution of one full step forward or back, or in the case of a step through kick, it means kicking with the rear foot and planting that foot forward or kicking with the forward foot and planting that foot back.

STRIKE -- the delivery of natural body weapons in hitting human targets, the method of which excludes punches and kicks.

SWITCH -- is changing from one stance or position to another while in place. This is done while moving the feet from one spot to another. This involves a lead leg where one of two things can happen, (a) you can step back then move forward, (b) step forward then move back, or a third possibility (c) jumping in place.

TAILORING -- fitting moves to your body size, makeup and strength, in order to maximize your physical efforts.

TRANSITIONAL RESPONSE -- instantaneously evolving from one position to another for purpose of offense or defense.

UNINTENTIONAL MOVES -- accidental and unplanned moves by an opponent which, when checked or not anticipated, can defeat your purpose. It is a normal reaction by an opponent.

WEIGHT DISTRIBUTION -- the apportionment of weight related to a particular stance. It may vary, fifty-fifty, sixty-forty, ninety-ten, etc.

"WITH" -- a very useful word in our Kenpo vocabulary which is adhered to by the more adept. It involves duel movements and eliminates the word "and" employing this principle eliminates wasted motion and economizes on time.

To order additional Ed Parker Sr.
books, please contact us at:

Kam IV, Inc./ Ed Parker Sr.
P.O. Box 595
South Pasadena, CA 91030

or

e-mail: kam_four@yahoo.com

CPSIA information can be obtained at www.ICGtesting.com
Printed in the USA
BVOW022205291211

279472BV00004B/4/P

The Magic Paintbrush

Robin Muller

DATE DUE	

SCHOLASTIC CANADA LTD.
New York Toronto London Auckland Sydney
Mexico City New Delhi Hong Kong Buenos Aires

Scholastic Canada Ltd.
175 Hillmount Road, Markham, Ontario L6C 1Z7, Canada
Scholastic Inc.
555 Broadway, New York, NY 10012, USA
Scholastic Australia Pty Limited
PO Box 579, Gosford, NSW 2250, Australia
Scholastic New Zealand Limited
Private Bag 94407, Greenmount, Auckland, New Zealand
Scholastic Ltd.
Villiers House, Clarendon Avenue, Leamington Spa,
Warwickshire CV32 5PR, UK

National Library of Canada Cataloguing in Publication

Muller, Robin
The magic paintbrush / Robin Muller.

ISBN 0-439-97432-1

I. Title.
PS8576.U424M34 2003   jC813'.54   C2002-905539-3
PZ7

6 5 4 3 2 1   Printed in Canada   03 04 05 06

To Sara and Melanie Irvine
and
to my brother Lawrence, who
gave me my first paintbrush

Long ago there lived an orphan boy called Nib. He couldn't read, he couldn't write, he couldn't even tell you how old he was. But he did know how to draw, and that was good, because more than anything else in the world, he wanted to be an artist.

Nib was so poor that he couldn't afford pens or brushes or paints. Instead, he followed the charcoal burner's cart that rumbled and bounced through the cobbled streets, and picked up the little black sticks that fell out.

With these charcoal sticks, Nib sketched on scraps of crates and boxes that piled up behind the market. Once he found a broken pencil in the gutter. When he sharpened it, it smelled of cedar, and the hard black lead tasted cold and sweet. On the back of a poster that had blown from a wall Nib drew a picture of a seagull, carefully shading in every feather and claw, finishing with its bright, mischievous eye.

He gazed with delight at his work. "One day," Nib cried, "I will make pictures so real that people will think they are alive."

During the day Nib did odd jobs to pay for the bowl of thin soup that kept him alive, but in the evening he hung around the outdoor cafés, listening to the artists arguing with each other over endless glasses of wine. When the final bottle was drained, the last candle flame was snuffed and the streets were wrapped in a velvet shadow, Nib made his way home to the bridge by the river.

One night, as he picked his way through the gloom, he was startled by a terrible cry, then another, followed by the heavy thuds of a cudgel. The cry came again, more desperate and painful, followed by more blows and muffled curses.

Nib was terrified, and shrank deeper into the shadow, but something about the helplessness and pain in the cry for help pierced his heart. Without thinking, Nib darted toward the sound, knocking over a bucket in his haste. It boomed in the darkness. Seizing a stick, Nib thumped the bucket and shouted at the top of his lungs: "C'mon, lads, let's get 'em!" He raced forward as though he had a gang of river rats at his heels, eager to pound the living daylights out of anyone foolish enough to get in their way.

Ahead of him Nib could hear the clash of hobnail boots fleeing down the alley. Crumpled against the wall he found a very old man, his face waxen in the dim light. "Thank you," the man gasped. "Those men, they would have killed me."

"It's all right," said Nib. "You're safe now."

At his refuge under the bridge Nib gently tended the old man. The other poor waifs who sheltered there offered their tattered rags to bandage his cuts, and Sara the watercress girl, who had saved one small bunch for her supper, gave it to the old man so he would have something fresh to eat. Warmed by the children's kindness, he went to sleep.

The next day Nib helped the old man back to his home, a lonely garret at the top of a rickety stair. Nib lit a candle and peered around. Books and scrolls filled the cupboards and shelves, cloths embroidered with strange letters hung from the ceiling, and the working table was covered with pens and pots of coloured ink.

Nib puzzled over the writing and the intricate decorations. "Are you an artist?" he asked shyly. His question was greeted with a laugh.

"In a way, yes. But not in the way you mean. I inscribe words — secret words — and make them beautiful. But pictures of this world I do not make."

"I want to be an artist," said Nib fervently. "I want to paint pictures so real that people will think they are alive!"

The old man looked at Nib thoughtfully. "Do you?" he said. "Then I shall help you." He shuffled among his boxes and chests and then pulled open a small drawer. "Ah, here it is!"

He held up an intricately carved wooden box and pressed a small clasp. The lid popped open to reveal a palette, rows of paint tablets and one beautiful red paintbrush with golden hairs.

"This, my little friend, is for you." He held out the box. "The brush has been used to adorn the Words of Life, and the power of life is in its touch. It will help you make pictures while you see with your eyes. But one day you will learn to see with your heart, and then you will no longer have need of it."

Nib was speechless with wonder. "Take it, take it!" insisted the old man. "It is small return for your kindness." Nib accepted the box and stuttered his thanks, almost fearing the old man would change his mind.

"Don't thank me, little one! Just remember that our lives, this world and everything in it is the gift. Let your pictures be the thanks."

As Nib hurried down the street, he had the odd sensation that the world was changing around him. He glanced back to the old man's garret, but it was gone. A stone wall stood where moments before he had descended a stair.

"I must be dreaming," he said, and clutched the box ever more tightly. At least that was real. He hurried back to his home under the bridge.

Nib smoothed out his picture of the seagull and opened the paint box. "Now I can finish you." Carefully he brushed in the colours. They seemed to flow and shade by themselves. The bird was beginning to look real. Soon everything was complete except for the little spot of brightness on the eye. Holding his breath and biting his lip, Nib touched a tiny dab of white on the spot. "There . . ." he murmured.

With a squawk and a terrific flurry of wings, the gull burst off the page — bowling Nib over in its flight. The sheet before him was empty. High above the bird circled, flying freely in the grey sky.

Sara, the watercress girl, heard the commotion and ran over. She gazed at the blank paper. "Nib," she said, "what happened to your picture of the seagull?"

Nib smiled and looked in wonder at the paintbrush.

The next day in the market square, Nib settled down beside a flower stall. With his paint box beside him and a board balanced on his knees, he gazed at a freshly blooming rose. The petals curled open with a crimson blush and drops of dew clung to the stem.

Nib touched his brush to the colours and then to the board. As he worked, the rose seemed to rise from the surface of the wood. Finally Nib dotted in the spots of light on the dew drops — and the flower tumbled to the ground!

"That boy just made the picture of a flower come to life!" shouted a bystander. "Impossible!" shouted another. "Do it again!" yelled yet another.

Nib did. He made a cat come to life, a dove, two pigs, a dozen chickens and another rose. An excited crowd gathered around him. "Do it again! Do it again!"

Suddenly a hand grasped his shoulder. Nib tried to wriggle free but it was no use. The hand belonged to Zagal, Captain of the King's Guard.

"I've been watching you, my little man," he growled, "and I know someone who would like to see that little trick of yours. Pick up your things, you're coming with me!"

Nib was taken to a massive grey building, dragged down a long dark hall and thrust into an enormous room.

He had never imagined anything like it. The floor was marble, velvet curtains framed the windows, delicate vases stood on polished black cabinets, and the walls were hung with rows of magnificent paintings.

"What have you brought me, Zagal?" demanded an irritated voice. A tall, elegantly dressed man turned toward them. It was the King. "What is this street urchin doing here?" he asked coldly.

"Forgive me, Your Majesty, but this boy did the most amazing thing. I saw him painting a flower — and the very moment he finished it, it came to life." Zagal pulled the rose Nib had painted from his pocket. "Then he painted a cat, a dove, pigs, some chickens. And they all come to life!" Zagal waved to his attendants and the animals Nib had painted were herded into the room.

"You imbecile!" screamed the King as a terrified chicken landed on his head. "How dare you bring a barnyard into my chambers!"

"Give me but a moment, Your Majesty," pleaded Zagal, "and I will prove that what I say is true."

Zagal thrust Nib down in front of a jade lion that stood on a nearby table. "Paint that, boy, or you will be sorry you were ever born!"

Nervously Nib studied the little statue. Then he opened his box and began to paint. "Not bad," muttered the King, as the brush danced over the board. "The boy has talent."

"Wait!" whispered Zagal. "Just wait!" A few minutes later Nib brushed in the final details of the jade lion. The instant he did so, it tumbled from the board and onto his lap.

"Let me see that!" snapped the King. He held the jade lion up to the light, then stared at Nib. "Well, my little artist," he said, "isn't it lucky that fate has brought you to me? We will be friends, great friends."

"Yes, Your Majesty. That would be nice," said Nib. "But please may I go home now?"

The King looked at him in astonishment, and then he burst out laughing. "Go? You will never go! You are far too precious. You will stay here with me — making the things I crave."

"No!" cried Nib. "You already have everything anybody could want! You don't need my help. Let me go home!"

The King seized Nib by the collar. "You will do as I say," he hissed. "Zagal, take this guttersnipe to the dungeons and lock him up. A night spent in the company of rats may help him change his mind."

The dungeon was dark and cold, and rats scurried between Nib's feet, but he didn't mind. As soon as the guards were gone, Nib took out his brush. Colours swirled and danced as he painted a roaring fire, a comfortable chair, flowers to sweeten the air, and a table piled high with food. "Not bad," he sniffed, mimicking the King. "Not bad at all."

The next morning, after breakfast, the King announced, "That young rascal must be so terrified and hungry that he will agree to anything. I will pay him a visit so he can see how forgiving I can be."

The door to the dungeon was thrown open, but when the King looked in and saw how comfortable Nib had made it, he screamed with rage. "Guards, seize the prisoner, beat him, cage him, load him with chains!" But before they could lay hands on him, Nib was gone. He had painted a tunnel and escaped. The guards squeezed into the tunnel, but they became hopelessly stuck.

"Search the city!" bellowed the King. "Every gutter and attic. And don't stop till you find him!"

Nib was in great danger. Everywhere the King's guards were waiting to arrest him. Posters appeared throughout the kingdom offering huge rewards for the capture of the boy who could bring pictures to life.

Nib sat by the road and gazed sadly at his paint box. "Perhaps I should throw you away," he said. "I can never use you without being caught." But then he had an idea. "I will go on painting, but I won't finish my pictures. Then they won't come to life."

As a travelling artist Nib journeyed from town to town. He painted fantastic castles perched on the sides of mountains, and busy ports where tall ships arrived with exotic fruit, coloured birds and strange animals. Rich and famous people begged him to paint portraits of them, offering fortunes for his services. But with every picture Nib never forgot to leave out some little detail, so his secret would not be revealed.

Nib should have been happy, but he wasn't. He could paint beautiful scenes better than anyone, but the more he looked for beauty, the more he found pain and ugliness. He saw huge factories built in pleasant meadows, little country towns swallowed by cities and turned into slums, and gentle animals beaten and neglected by their owners.

Disheartened, Nib sat down by a brook which had been poisoned by a factory's waste. "The paintbrush is magic," he said to himself. "Maybe I can paint it better." Setting up his easel, he painted a clear babbling stream. But every stroke became muddy and black. "The brush will only let me paint what I see with my eyes," he sighed unhappily, "not what I see with my heart."

Lonely and sad, Nib returned to the city to find the friends he had lived with under the bridge. But when he arrived at his old home, no one was there.

He strolled over to the square where he had first painted the rose. He gazed fondly at the crowds and the buildings — and then caught sight of a familiar figure huddled in a doorway. It was Sara the watercress girl, but she was so different from when he had known her. Her face was thin and pinched, and a strange brightness was in her eyes.

"Sara, what has happened to you?" Nib cried.

"Oh, Nib!" the girl replied. "Palace guards came looking for you. They drove us out of our place under the bridge and burnt all our things. We had to sleep wherever we could — and I got sick. Help me, Nib, I'm so hungry and cold." She collapsed on the ground coughing.

"Sara, Sara, I'm sorry," cried Nib. Quickly he opened his box and painted a beautiful woollen shawl and tucked it around her shoulders. Then he painted a bowl full of oranges, pears and grapes. But Sara was too weak to eat.

"I will paint you well!" he said desperately. "It will work — it *must* work." And he began to paint the girl's portrait, not as she was, but healthy and happy, with clear eyes and rosy cheeks.

It was no use. With every stroke the colours darkened and cracked. "It's all my fault," he cried pitifully. "I wish I had never taken the old man's gift." Tears ran down his cheeks and splashed onto the picture. As they did so, something wondrous began to happen. The colours suddenly brightened, filling the portrait with light, and when Nib looked up, Sara was standing before him, smiling.

"You're well again!" he cried joyously. "Everything is going to be all right!"

"It certainly is!" a wicked voice bellowed behind him. Nib was yanked to his feet and twisted around. He found himself looking into the cruel eyes of Zagal. "I knew that one day you would return to your little friend here. All I had to do was keep watch. Now you're both coming with me!"

At the palace the King was delighted to see Nib. "So, my little artist," he crowed, "you tried to escape me. How foolish of you! It won't happen again, I assure you."

The King smiled and rubbed his hands together. "I have some work for you to do. And if you refuse, you will force me to be nasty to your little friend here." He waved at Sara. "Very, very nasty."

Day after day, Nib sat in the gallery, painting pearls, sapphires, gold doubloons, bars of silver. The King never tired of watching him, and took a childish pleasure in counting the treasure as it fell from Nib's board. "Soon I will be rich enough to pay for anything I want — even the biggest army in the world," he gloated.

Nib was terrified at the thought, but the King's boast gave him an idea. "Your Majesty," he began, "instead of painting gold and jewels, why don't I just paint what you want and you shall have it?"

"But what if it's something really big, like a fleet of warships?"

"I can paint that!" said Nib eagerly. "I can paint big things on the wall, and you can just walk into the picture. I'll show you."

Standing on a chair, Nib started to paint. The brush flew in his hand as he went: oak hulls, tall masts, brass fittings, rows of shining cannons. Soon a fleet of magnificent warships seemed to be moored only a short distance away. Finally Nib painted a gangplank leading right onto the deck of the nearest ship.

"The royal navy, Your Majesty. Please step aboard."

The King looked warily at the picture. Everything looked normal. Sailors were coiling ropes and the vessels were gently rising on the tide.

"Very well, I shall." He ordered Zagal and all his men to follow him on board. From the deck he called out, "This is marvellous. With these ships I can conquer the world. Paint me a breeze so we can set sail."

Nib painted the sails beginning to fill with wind. "More, more!" shouted the King. Nib worked furiously. Soon the peaceful sea started to dance as he painted wave after wave. Still the King yelled for more. Under Nib's brush the clear blue sky turned grey, fluffy white clouds turned black, and foam leapt from the crest of the waves.

"Enough!" screamed the King, but Nib's brush still flew. The sun disappeared behind a cloud and thunder shook the sky. The King's cries were almost drowned as the fleet began to be swept out to sea. "Enough! Stop this at once!"

"All right," yelled Nib over the din of the storm. "I *will* stop! I don't need this brush to paint my pictures." And, seizing his paint box and brush, he hurled them into the raging water.

"Scoundrel!" screamed the King. Suddenly there was a blinding flash of lightning and a terrible crash. The King, the fleet and the sea were gone. Nib was staring at a blank wall.

Without the King, life in the country improved. Soon the meadows were filled with wild flowers, and the rivers ran fresh and sweet. One day, Nib and Sara were happily strolling through the city when something caught Nib's eye. He stooped to pick up a little black stick from between the cobbles. He rolled it gently in his fingers, and on a piece of paper sketched Sara's portrait. "The best pictures," he laughed as he looked at her smiling face, "are the ones you make with your heart."